CONTEMPORARY'S

EDGE ON ENGLISH

GRAMMAR
Write Away
BOOK 2

BETSY RUBIN

Project Editor
Patricia Reid

McGraw Hill **Wright Group**

Library of Congress Cataloging-in-Publication Data

Rubin, Betsy.
   Grammar write away : book 2 / Betsy Rubin : project editor,
Patricia Reid.
      p.   cm.—(Contemporary's edge on English)
   ISBN 0-8092-4806-9
   1. English language—Grammar—1950-   2. English language—
Examinations, questions, etc.   I. Reid, Patricia.   II. Title.
III. Series.
PE1112.R78   1988   88-39766
428.2—dc19   CIP

Wright Group

ISBN: 0-8092-4806-9

Send all inquiries to:
Wright Group/McGraw-Hill
130 East Randolph Street, Suite 400
Chicago, Illinois 60601

Printed in the United States of America.

23 24 25 26 27 28 DBH 09 08 07 06

The **McGraw·Hill** Companies

CONTENTS

TO THE INSTRUCTOR

Grammar Write Away Book 2 is the second book of a two-volume set dealing with common grammar and writing problems. Both books are designed for use either inside the classroom or for independent study. While an instructor will need to check students' original sentences and paragraphs, students can check most of their own work using the answer key at the end of the book.

ASSUMPTIONS

This book assumes that grammar instruction is most useful when it is taught in the context of *writing*. That is, in order for students to learn and to use grammatical rules, they need to apply them directly by writing their own sentences and paragraphs. Fill-in-the-blank exercises, while a useful focusing tool, are not an end in themselves; students must have the opportunity to use what they have learned in their own original writing. Throughout the book students are asked to write short paragraphs using what they have practiced.

Another assumption is that grammar is best learned in a *context*. This allows students to see how grammar works in real situations; it also makes grammar instruction more interesting and meaningful. For this reason, *Grammar Write Away* uses real-life themes such as child rearing, teen problems, and work situations in its lessons.

A third assumption is that grammar instruction must be *practical*. Grammatical rules are not learned for their own sakes, but rather for their utility in helping students write good sentences and paragraphs. Thus, this book presents the minimum rules necessary using simple and clear terminology.

The final assumption of *Grammar Write Away* is that students need to learn standard English grammar for academic and occupational success. Thus, the activities in this book are writing, rather than speaking, activities. The instructor may wish, however, to show applications to speaking in formal situations.

At the same time, the instructor should never tell a student that his or her style of speech is "wrong" or "bad." There are many varieties of spoken English, all of which are both acceptable and valued in informal conversation with family and friends. The instructor needs to point out merely that a certain style is *appropriate* in some situations and inappropriate in others.

SCOPE

Grammar Write Away Book 2 addresses students who are working with basic grammar and writing issues. Attention is given to the following areas:

- How to construct a correct simple sentence, including simple sentences with compound elements
- How to construct correct compound and complex sentences
- How to avoid fragments and run-ons
- How to use different parts of speech—nouns, pronouns, adjectives, and adverbs
- How to use verb tenses—present, past, future, present perfect, and past perfect—as well as the continuous aspect
- How to make verbs agree with subjects
- How to make pronouns agree with antecedents
- How to use commas and semicolons correctly
- How to use adjective clauses and modifiers correctly

FORMAT

1. Most lessons begin with a sample sentence that illustrates a principle or a common error.
2. In the "Insight" section, students are led through a step-by-step analysis of a particular grammar issue. Sometimes an incorrect sentence is used as an example, and students are asked to find the problem. This analysis leads to a simple, easy-to-follow rule.

3. Next, students complete "Practice" exercises that range from controlled and easy (e.g., fill in the blank) to freer and more difficult (e.g., students generate their own sentences). "Proofread" exercises are designed to encourage students to locate and correct errors embedded in paragraphs or longer passages.

4. Special exercises ("Show What You Know") are interspersed throughout the book. Most of these are writing assignments on interesting topics and require students to use a variety of principles they have learned. While explicit review lessons are included where necessary, the "Show What You Knows" should also be regarded as an important form of cumulative review.

5. A 50-point diagnostic test is included at the beginning of this book to help the instructor determine where students need particular study. An evaluation chart at the end of the diagnostic test correlates questions on the test to sections in this book.

6. A 100-point final test appears at the end in order to determine students' progress. An evaluation chart also accompanies this test.

7. The back of the book contains an appendix that provides lists of verbs with irregular past-tense forms and with irregular past participles.

APPROACH

Because many lessons build on previous practice, students should work through the entire book. If a particular lesson is especially easy, it may be done quickly but should not be skipped.

In the classroom setting, the instructor should write the lesson's opening example on the blackboard and guide students through its analysis according to the steps of the "Insight" section. Students should then go over this section on their own and begin the exercises. For independent study, students can work through the lessons entirely on their own.

Students can check their own answers in the back of the book. Correct answers are given for controlled exercises, and suggestions are made for some of the freer exercises in which students write their own sentences. In any case, the instructor should be sure to check students' original writing.

In checking sentences and paragraphs, the instructor needs to focus on the point at hand and on previously taught material only. The instructor should not be overly concerned with errors students have not yet learned how to correct.

It should be noted that this book focuses on grammar skills, not writing skills. While the students are expected to use a standard paragraph format, they are not asked to write formal paragraphs or compositions. Issues such as stating the controlling idea or providing support, though they are important skills that good writers must develop, are not covered in this book.

In addition to assigning "Show What You Know" and other review exercises, the instructor may wish to present his or her own short, periodic quizzes. As mentioned earlier, a final test appears at the end of the book.

A FINAL WORD

The successful application of rules to improve a student's grammar and writing requires time and effort on the part of both the student and the instructor. This process can be both interesting and enjoyable when viewed as a challenge and as the bridge to better communication.

TO THE STUDENT

Why Is Grammar Important?

Mr. Davis has placed an ad for a sales position at his insurance company. Sonia Wilson has seen the ad and is sure she is right for the job. She sends this letter to Mr. Davis:

Dear Mr. Davis:

I am writin this letter to apply for the advertised position at your company. The position as sales trainee. I feel I would be well qualified for this job. Because I had a great deal of background. In the area of sales. As a clerical assistant at the Western Insurance Company, working closely with experienced sales personnel. I loved my job, I been there for two years, although, I am looking for a position with more challenge and able to advance.

My résumé is enclosed which includes further information about my academic and professional background. A list of references are available upon request I looking forward to hearing from you. Thank you for you're interest.

Sincerely,
Sonia N. Wilson

Mr. Davis notes with favor that Ms. Wilson has had some experience in the field, and he is impressed by her enthusiasm. However, he is shocked by her grammar.

It is hard for him to follow this letter because he can't tell where one idea starts and another ends. Some of the sentences seem short and choppy while others drag on and on. Several words are used incorrectly.

Worst of all, from Mr. Davis's point of view, is that he cannot tell if she is still working at the Western Insurance Company or not. Mr. Davis starts to wonder if Ms. Wilson made this point fuzzy on purpose. Perhaps she has something to hide. Without another thought, he places her letter in the file marked "Reject."

Sonia Wilson has been misjudged. She is, in fact, a bright and honest person who is eager to advance in her career. As she writes, she knows what she is trying to say, but she has not stopped to think about how her writing appears to the reader—in this case a potential employer. Her poor grammar and writing skills, which have led Mr. Davis to misjudge her, are the major barriers to her success.

Ms. Wilson is not alone. Many men and women have problems with formal grammar and writing. If you know *you* need to improve your grammar and writing, you have already taken the first step. You have identified the problem. Now, use *Grammar Write Away Book 2* to solve it!

Practical Lessons

The lessons in this book give you easy-to-follow rules that you can apply *right away* to improve your writing. The rules are there to be used—not just learned for their own sake!

Here are a few suggestions for using the book. First, work through all the lessons, even if some seem easy to you. They may help you with more difficult lessons later on.

Read carefully each sample sentence or paragraph appearing at the beginning of a lesson. Then work through the "Insight" questions, which will help you to understand the rules. Be sure to study the rule box, which summarizes the information you have just studied.

Now work through *all* the exercises. The "Practice" exercises will help you use the rules correctly. With many exercises, you will need to write out the answers on your own paper. The "Proofread" exercises will help you sharpen your proofreading skills so that you will get used to correcting your own writing. As you work on the exercises, feel free to look back to the rule box.

After you do each exercise, check it over carefully. Many of the worst grammar mistakes are simply careless errors!

Finally, after doing *each* exercise, check your answers in the back of the book. If you get every answer correct, you can feel justifiably proud. If you find a mistake, don't lose hope! First correct the error and then take a moment to figure out *why* you made it in the first place. This way, you'll be more likely to avoid making the same mistake the next time you start to write.

Every so often, you'll have the chance to do a special exercise—"Show What You Know." In many of these exercises, you'll write a paragraph or a short paper on an interesting topic. This way, you'll get a chance to express your ideas and use good grammar, too. If you're working in a class, your instructor will read these paragraphs and may ask you to share them with your fellow students. If you're working on your own, try to find someone knowledgeable about grammar to check over your work.

At the back of the book, the Appendix contains a list of irregular verbs. Refer to the Appendix whenever necessary as you work through the book.

A Note About Good Grammar

Everyone uses different styles of English for different occasions. No one speaks to his oldest friends the way he speaks at a job interview. No one writes a letter to her grandmother the same way she writes a job application letter.

Informal speech and writing are not "wrong." They can, however, be *inappropriate* in certain situations. There are times when you will need to use standard English, and *Grammar Write Away Book 2* will help you with this. Now look at what this book could do for Ms. Wilson's letter:

Dear Mr. Davis:

    I am writing this letter to apply for the advertised position as sales trainee at your company. I feel I would be well qualified for this job because of my extensive background in the area of insurance sales. As a clerical assistant at the Western Insurance Company for the past two years, I have had the opportunity to work closely with experienced sales personnel. Although my job at Western is satisfying, I am looking for a position with more challenge and more opportunities for advancement.

    Enclosed is my résumé, which includes further information about my academic and professional background. In addition, a list of references is available upon request. I look forward to hearing from you. Thank you for your interest.

Sincerely,
Sonia N. Wilson

Now Ms. Wilson has her chance for success! You can, too. Good luck in your efforts.

PREVIEW TEST

This test covers the main points you will study in this book. Different people have different strengths and weaknesses in grammar, and this short test will help you evaluate yours. There are fifty questions in all. Don't worry about how long you take to answer them. If you do not know the answer to a question, skip it and move on.

Remember that this test is only to help you determine where you need to concentrate in this book. After you have taken the test, check your answers on page 10. The evaluation chart on page 11 will tell you which chapters in this book you need to concentrate on.

For questions 1–20, read and answer each question. Be sure to read each answer choice carefully before you make your choice. Circle one answer only.

1. Which is *not* a complete sentence?

   a. Explain this, please.
   b. He is confused.
   c. A lack of comprehension on his part.
   d. Does he comprehend the lesson?

2. Read the sentence below. Then choose the correct sentence to follow it.

   Students often fail to participate in class.

   a. First, boredom with the lesson.
   b. One reason is boredom.
   c. The first reason: boredom.
   d. Both a and b are correct.

3. Which sentence uses commas correctly?

   a. Students must be motivated, diligent, and prepared.
   b. Students should pay attention in class, and ask tough questions.
   c. Motivated instructors look, learn and, listen carefully to their students.
   d. Both a and b are correct.

4. Which sentence is *not* correct?

   a. Our school is a fascinating place, there are students here from many different backgrounds.
   b. Our school is a fascinating place there are students here from many different backgrounds.
   c. Both sentences are correct.
   d. Both sentences are incorrect.

5. Read the two sentences below. How could they be combined correctly?

   The grammar is easy. The vocabulary is difficult.

   a. The grammar is easy. But, the vocabulary is difficult.
   b. While the grammar is easy, the vocabulary is difficult.
   c. The grammar is easy, however the vocabulary is difficult.
   d. All are correct.

6. Which transition best fits in the following pair of sentences?

Different test types are appropriate for different subjects. _____, essay tests are commonly used in English classes.

   a. In addition   **b.** For instance   **c.** In short   **d.** One example is

7. Read the two sentences below. How could they be combined correctly?

I have decided to return to school. I wish to complete my studies.

   a. I have decided to return to school. Because I wish to complete my studies.
   b. Because I wish to complete my studies, I have decided to return to school.
   c. I have decided to return to school because, I wish to complete my studies.
   d. Both a and c are correct.

8. Which item is *not* correct?

   a. My education is my priority, therefore I will only work part-time this semester.
   b. My education is my priority; therefore, I will only work part-time this semester.
   c. My education is my priority. Therefore, I will only work part-time this semester.
   d. Both a and b are incorrect.

9. Which word belongs in the sentence below?

_____ many of today's high schools are overcrowded, some young people are able to find the attention they need.

   a. Because   **b.** Although   **c.** However   **d.** Therefore

10. Which word belongs in the sentence below?

Some students do poorly in high school, _____ they succeed in the world of work.

   a. but   **b.** yet   **c.** however   **d.** Both a and b are correct.

11. The military careers presentation was given by _____.

   a. Captain Falkenberg
   b. captain Falkenberg
   c. a captain
   d. Both a and c are correct.

12. Several fine schools have a majority of _____ in the student body.

   a. womans   **b.** womens   **c.** women   **d.** woman

13. An _____ high school record is scrutinized.

   a. applicant   **b.** applicants   **c.** applicant's   **d.** applicants'

14. His or her _____ are rigorously checked.

   a. reference   **b.** references   **c.** reference's   **d.** references'

15. Do you know if the school offers _____ financial aid?

   a. many   **b.** much   **c.** a number of   **d.** Both a and b are correct.

(continued)

16. _____ received our diplomas last spring.

    a. My sister and I   **c.** Me and my sister
    b. My sister and me   **d.** Both a and b are correct.

17. Send the grades to _____.

    a. my husband and me   **c.** my husband and myself
    b. my husband and I   **d.** Both a and c are correct.

18. The students seemed _____ to participate.

    a. very eager   **c.** real eager
    b. very eagerly   **d.** real eagerly

19. _____ tuition and expenses did not go up much.

    a. They   **b.** They're   **c.** There   **d.** Their

20. At the end of the term, they wrote _____ than ever before.

    a. more clear   **c.** more clearer
    b. more clearly   **d.** more clearlier

For the paragraph below, choose the correct verb form for each sentence. Circle one answer only.

       Several months ago, Julian started attending evening school.

He _____21_____ to study word processing. He currently _____22_____ school three evenings per week. Recently, his instructor _____23_____ him for all of the hard work he _____24_____. Julian, needless to say, is quite pleased. Back in his old high school, he _____25_____ only criticism. For years he _____26_____ to find some encouragement. Julian looks forward to his graduation day. When he receives his competency certificate, he _____27_____ a proud man.

21. **a.** began
    b. begun
    c. had began
    d. had begun

22. **a.** attending
    b. attended
    c. attends
    d. attend

23. **a.** has praise
    b. has praised
    c. had praise
    d. had praised

24. **a.** have been done
    b. has been done
    c. have been doing
    d. has been doing

25. **a.** had heard
    b. had heared
    c. has heard
    d. has heared

26. **a.** had been try
    b. had been trying
    c. had been tried
    d. had trying

27. **a.** be
    b. is
    c. will be
    d. going to be

For questions 28–32, read and answer each question. Circle one answer only.

28. She _____ learned nothing about her grades so far.

   a. ain't   **b.** hasn't   **c.** haven't   **d.** has

29. If she knew her grades, she _____ less nervous now.

   a. would be   **b.** will be   **c.** be   **d.** were

30. Circle the letter of the correct sentence.

   a. I'm a little anxious, she said.
   b. "I'm a little anxious" she said.
   c. "I'm a little anxious," she said.
   d. "I'm a little anxious, she said."

31. Circle the letter of the correct sentence.

   a. "I am concerned, she said, because I don't know my grades."
   b. "I am concerned" she said "because I don't know my grades."
   c. "I am concerned," she said, "because I don't know my grades."
   d. "I am concerned," she said. "Because I don't know my grades."

32. Circle the letter of the correct sentence.

   a. Yesterday I asked her "why was she worried about her grades"?
   b. Yesterday I asked her why are you worried about your grades?
   c. Yesterday I asked her why was she worried about her grades.
   d. Yesterday I asked her why she was worried about her grades.

(*continued*)

For the paragraph below, choose the correct word for each space. Circle one answer only.

Here _____ an example of a successful nontraditional school. The
      33

women's prison offers a special GED program for _____ inmates.
                       34

Overwhelmingly, the students who attend this program _____ satisfied
                                  35

with the quality of the classes. Most of the students _____ to do well.
                                  36

Success in class _____ the first goal on the way to success in the outside
                37

world. For this reason, each of the students _____ the opportunity to
                       38

attend special tutoring sessions to supplement _____ classes. At the end
                       39

of each six-week term, the teachers or the warden herself _____
                       40

certificates of completion. The news about this program _____ not all
                       41

good, however. The prison governing committee _____ not give
                42

education a high priority.

33. a. be
   b. are
   c. is
   d. Both a and b are correct.

34. a. its
   b. their
   c. her
   d. his or her

35. a. are
   b. is
   c. feels
   d. Both b and c are correct.

36. a. want
   b. wants
   c. wanted
   d. Both a and b are correct.

37. a. are
   b. is
   c. constitutes
   d. Both b and c are correct.

38. a. has
   b. have
   c. receive
   d. Both b and c are correct.

39. a. their
   b. your
   c. her
   d. his or her

40. a. award
   b. awards
   c. presents
   d. Both b and c are correct.

41. a. are
   b. is
   c. is or are
   d. ain't

42. a. does
   b. do
   c. have done
   d. Both b and c are correct.

For questions 43–50, read and answer each question. Circle one answer only.

43. Which word is *not* correct in the sentence?

That is the instructor _____ teaches accounting.

   a. which   **b.** who   **c.** that   **d.** All are correct.

44. Which sentence is correct?

    a. The course is excellent which covers American history.
    b. The course which covers American history is excellent.
    c. It is excellent the course that covers American history.
    d. Both a and b are correct.

45. Which verb form is correct for the sentence?

Paul Greenberg is an instructor who always _____ test papers promptly.

    a. grade
    b. do grade
    c. grades
    d. Both a and b are correct.

46. Choose the correct way to complete the sentence below.

In the desk, _____

    a. Ms. McKenzie put away her notebook.
    b. I watched Ms. McKenzie put away her notebook.
    c. Ms. McKenzie's notebook was hidden beneath a pile of papers.
    d. I wondered how I could find out my grade.

47. Choose the correct way to complete the sentence below.

Explaining each point clearly, _____.

    a. the students were able to follow Professor Anaya's economics lecture.
    b. Professor Anaya lectured about the different economic systems.
    c. I listened carefully to Professor Anaya's lecture about the different economic systems.
    d. All are correct.

48. Choose the correct way to complete the sentence below.

Ms. Michalski is _____.

    a. dedicated, intelligent, and effective.
    b. a dedicated teacher, intelligent, and teaches effectively.
    c. a dedicated, intelligent, and effective teacher.
    d. Both a and c are correct.

49. Which sentence is correct?

    a. The man that lives next door to me, is a retired professor.
    b. The man, that lives next door to me is a retired professor.
    c. The man, that lives next door to me, is a retired professor.
    d. The man that lives next door to me is a retired professor.

50. Which sentence is correct?

    a. Dr. Farlow who now quietly gardens all day, once taught nuclear physics.
    b. Dr. Farlow, who now quietly gardens all day once taught nuclear physics.
    c. Dr. Farlow, who now quietly gardens all day, once taught nuclear physics.
    d. Dr. Farlow who now quietly gardens all day once taught nuclear physics.

Answers start on page 10.

Preview Test Answer Key

1. **c** A lack of comprehension on his part.
2. **b** One reason is boredom.
3. **a** Students must be motivated, diligent, and prepared.
4. **d** Both sentences are incorrect.
5. **b** While the grammar is easy, the vocabulary is difficult.
6. **b** For instance
7. **b** Because I wish to complete my studies, I have decided to return to school.
8. **a** My education is my priority, therefore I will only work part-time this semester.
9. **b** Although
10. **d** Both a and b (*but, yet*) are correct.
11. **d** Both a and c (*Captain Falkenberg, a captain*) are correct.
12. **c** women
13. **c** applicant's
14. **b** references
15. **b** much
16. **a** My sister and I
17. **a** my husband and me
18. **a** very eager
19. **d** Their
20. **b** more clearly
21. **a** began
22. **c** attends
23. **b** has praised
24. **d** has been doing
25. **a** had heard
26. **b** had been trying
27. **c** will be
28. **d** has
29. **a** would be
30. **c** "I'm a little anxious," she said.
31. **c** "I am concerned," she said, "because I don't know my grades."
32. **d** Yesterday I asked her why she was worried about her grades.
33. **c** is
34. **a** its
35. **a** are
36. **a** want
37. **d** Both b and c (*is, constitutes*) are correct.
38. **a** has
39. **c** her
40. **d** Both b and c (*awards, presents*) are correct.
41. **b** is
42. **a** does
43. **a** which
44. **b** The course which covers American history is excellent.
45. **c** grades
46. **c** Ms. McKenzie's notebook was hidden beneath a pile of papers.
47. **b** Professor Anaya lectured about the different economic systems.
48. **d** Both a and c are correct.
49. **d** The man that lives next door to me is a retired professor.
50. **c** Dr. Farlow, who now quietly gardens all day, once taught nuclear physics.

Preview Test Evaluation Chart

Use the chart below to determine the grammar skills in which you need to do the most work. Circle the items you answered correctly and pay particular attention to areas where you missed half or more of the questions.

Content Area	Item Number	Review Pages	Number Correct
Chapter 1 The simple sentence	1, 2, 3, 4	12–29	___/ 4
Chapter 2 Connecting sentences	5, 6, 7, 8 9, 10	32–55	___/ 6
Chapter 3 Nouns and pronouns	11, 12, 13, 14 15, 16, 17, 19	58–76	___/ 8
Adjectives and adverbs	18, 20	77–83	___/ 2
Chapter 4 Verb tenses	21, 22, 23, 24, 25, 26, 27	85–102	___/ 7
Chapter 5 Negatives	28	104–107	___/ 1
Conditional	29	108–110	___/ 1
Quoted and reported speech	30, 31, 32	111–116	___/ 3
Chapter 6 Subject-verb agreement	33, 35, 36, 37, 38, 40, 41, 42	118–130	___/ 8
Pronoun agreement	34, 39	133–137	___/ 2
Chapter 7 Adjective clauses	43, 44, 45	139–145	___/ 3
Misplaced and dangling modifiers	46, 47	147–151	___/ 2
Commas with modifiers	49, 50	152–155	___/ 2
Parallel structure	48	156–158	___/ 1
		Total	___/ 50

CHAPTER 1
THE SIMPLE SENTENCE

— Goals —

- To recognize complete sentences
- To find subjects and verbs in simple sentences
- To recognize compound subjects, verbs, and complements
- To recognize and correct fragments and run-ons

READING SENTENCES

Complete That Thought!

Read the passage below silently.

> I returned to school last year. More education was necessary for my career goals. In a few months, I will graduate and look for a job with a good company.

INSIGHT

This passage is easy to read and understand. It contains several clearly written sentences.

A *period* ⊡ signals the end of each sentence. How many sentences are in the paragraph? _____ sentences

You should have said three sentences because there are three periods. (Note: A comma ⊡ is different from a period. A comma does *not* signal the end of a sentence.)

What type of letter starts each sentence? a _____ letter

You're right if you said a capital letter.

Now copy each sentence on a separate line below. Remember the period at the end and the capital letter at the beginning.

1. _____

2. _____

3. _____

Now read the sentences again, but this time do it out loud. At the end of every sentence, your voice should go *down*, and you should *pause* before you go on to the next sentence.

> In writing, the end of a sentence is signaled by a period.
> In speaking, the end of a sentence is signaled by a pause.

Now take a look at the two sentences below.

> Why did you decide to go back to school?
> I wanted a job that paid more money!

Write the mark that ends the first sentence here: __. Write the mark that ends the second sentence here: __.

The first mark ? is called a **question mark**. It is used at the end of sentences that *ask* something. The second mark ! is called an **exclamation point**. It is used at the end of sentences that *exclaim* something—express a strong emotion.

A Common Problem

The passage below has some problems. Read it silently.

> I want. Have a good career. Family.

When you read all the words silently, can you understand the writer? _____ No! Did you find yourself wanting to ask, "*What* do you want? *Who* has a good career? *What about* a family?"

Now read the words out loud, remembering to pause after each period. Does each part sound normal and natural? _____ No, indeed! The "sentences" sound strange and choppy. This is because none of them express a complete idea. Now try reading this passage:

> I want to finish my education. I would like to have a good career. I also
> want to raise a family.

Did you find that these sentences answered the questions the original ones raised? That is because these sentences are *complete*; that is, they express complete ideas. In this chapter, you will learn what a sentence is—and what it is not. This will help you to write clear and intelligent sentences and paragraphs.

———————————————— PRACTICE ————————————————

Decide if each line below is a complete statement or not. Circle YES or NO. The first one has been done for you.

YES (NO) **1.** Wanted to go back.

YES NO **2.** I wanted to go back to school last fall.

YES NO **3.** I need a better-paying job.

YES NO **4.** After my GED.

YES NO **5.** After I get my GED, I want to start a family.

YES NO **6.** My wife and I love children.

YES NO **7.** Not getting any younger.

YES NO **8.** Children a yard.

Answers start on page 169.

SIMPLE SENTENCES

The Minimum Requirements

Every sentence must meet these minimum requirements:

- It must have a *subject*.
- It must have a *verb*.
- It must contain a *complete idea*.

A sentence may have more than these elements, but it cannot have less. A sentence with just one subject, verb, and complete idea is a **simple sentence**. Let's examine now these minimum requirements.

Subjects and Verbs

Steven operated the lathe carefully.

INSIGHT

The sentence above is a complete sentence, but exactly what is the subject and what is the verb? The **verb** shows the action of the sentence. The **subject** is the person or thing that performs the action.

Often it is easiest to look for the verb first. Go back to the sentence now and ask yourself, "What is the action?" What is the verb? _____ You are right if you wrote the word *operated*. *Operated* is the verb—the action—of the sentence.

Now look for the subject. Just ask yourself, "What person or thing performed this action?" In other words, *who* operated? What is the subject? _____ You are right again if you wrote the word *Steven*. *Steven* was the one who operated the lathe.

Be careful! The subject usually comes before the verb, but it is not always the first word of the sentence. Also, the subject and the verb are not always right next to each other. In the example below, underline the subject and the verb and label them with *S* and *V*.

All day long, Steven carefully operated the lathe.

If you marked *Steven* as the subject and *operated* as the verb, you were correct.

The verb shows the action of the sentence.
The subject is the person or thing that does the action.

BEING VERBS

We have said that the verb shows the action of the sentence. This is true most of the time, but some verbs do not actually show action. Here are some common examples:

Education **is** important.
You **seem** intelligent.
It **was** the answer.

The most common being verbs are *seem*, *remain*, *become*, *appear*, and any form of the verb *be* (*am*, *is*, *are*, *was*, or *were*).

──────────────────────── PRACTICE 1 ────────────────────────

Underline the subject and verb in each sentence. Label the subject with *S* and the verb with *V*. (You can start with either the subject or the verb, whichever is easiest for you to find first.) The first one has been done for you.

      S   V

1. Steven operated the lathe carefully.

2. He added oil regularly.

3. Every evening, Steven worked eight hours at the nail factory.

4. He seemed mature and responsible.

5. His foreman frequently checked the machine.

6. Fortunately, Steven was a careful and conscientious worker.

Answers start on page 169.

Complete Idea

    Sara fell.

INSIGHT

We have said that a sentence must express a complete idea. Sometimes a very short sentence, like the one above, expresses a complete idea.

Sometimes a subject and verb alone are not enough, as in the example below:

    Sara got.

Sara got *what*? This sentence does not contain a complete idea. A word or words need to be added to complete the idea:

    Sara got a sprained ankle.

The words *a sprained ankle* are used to complete the idea started by the words *Sara got*. The group of words used to complete the idea started by a subject and verb is called a **complement**. A complement can be long or short. Underline the complements in the sentences below:

    Sara got a sprained ankle yesterday.
    Sara got interested in cleaning the gutters after the bad storm last Sunday.

You're right if you underlined the words *a sprained ankle yesterday* and *interested in cleaning the gutters after the bad storm last Sunday*.

Sometimes a complement isn't necessary for a complete idea, but the writer has added one to give more information about the subject and verb. Look at the examples below:

    Sara fell.
    Sara fell off a tall ladder.

The complement, *off a tall ladder*, tells more about the subject and verb, *Sara fell*.

> A complete sentence must have a subject and a verb.
> A sentence must also tell a complete idea.
> Many, but not all, sentences require a complement after the verb
> to complete the idea.

──────────────── PRACTICE 2 ────────────────

Underline the subject and the verb in each sentence. If there is a complement, underline it too. (Don't worry about words before the subject or between the subject and verb.) Then label each with *S*, *V*, and *C*. The first one has been done for you.

      S   V   C

1. Sara cleaned the gutters on her roof yesterday.

2. To reach them, she climbed a ten-foot ladder.

3. Dead leaves clogged the gutters.

4. Sara thoroughly swept them all away.

5. Unfortunately, she stretched too far to get the corner.

6. Then she suddenly lost her balance.

7. She slipped.

──────────────── PRACTICE 3 ────────────────

In the following paragraph, underline the subject, verb, and complement (if any) in each sentence. Label with *S*, *V*, and *C*. Again, don't worry about words before the subject or between the subject and the verb.

     I dropped out of school at age fourteen. For years, I did odd jobs around the neighborhood. I stayed at my parents' house with my younger brothers and sisters. Eventually, I left. My income was too small for my own apartment. As a result, the streets became my home. Life got more and more difficult. Fortunately, my cousin kindly took me in. He found me a job at his factory. With his encouragement, I returned to school for my GED. Now I am on my way to better times.

Answers start on page 169.

NEGATIVES, QUESTIONS, COMMANDS

Don't Do What?

1. I do not care to discuss the matter.
2. Do you understand my point?
3. Please leave the premises immediately.

All of the above are complete sentences with subjects and verbs, but they are different kinds of sentences from those you have just been studying. Sentence 1 is a negative sentence, sentence 2 is a question, and sentence 3 is a command. In the following lesson, you will learn how to find the subjects and verbs in these types of sentences. First, let's do some more work on verbs.

Some Verbs Have Two Parts

Verbs often have different forms. For example, look at the changes in the verb *live*:

I **lived** alone last year.
I **live** with my cousin now.
I **will live** with him next year.

INSIGHT

The verb form changes when the ***tense***, or time period, changes from past to present to future. (You will learn more about verb tenses later in the book.)

Notice that sometimes there is more than one part to the verb. In the third sentence above, the verb has two parts: *will live*. The word *live* is the **main verb**. It carries the meaning. The word *will* is the **helping verb**; in other words, it helps out the main verb.

There are many different helping verbs. *Have*, *had*, *is*, and *was* are all often used as helping verbs.

> **Verbs can appear in different forms.**
> **Sometimes verbs have more than one part: one or more helping verbs**
> **and a main verb.**

PRACTICE 1

Underline the verb in each sentence. Underline *all parts*. Write *MV* over the main verb. If you see a helping verb, write *HV* over it. (There may be more than one helping verb, or there may be no helping verb at all.) The first one has been done for you.

```
   HV   HV   MV
```
1. I <u>have</u> <u>been</u> <u>living</u> with my cousin for a year.

2. I help him with the rent.

3. He helps me with my schoolwork.

4. I am working at a factory.

5. My cousin has been working there for several years.

6. We will look for new jobs next year.

7. We need more money and more challenge.

8. We have been having a hard time paying bills.

Answers start on page 169.

Negatives

1. I **do** not **eat** cauliflower.
2. They **did** not **inform** the landlord of their decision to paint the walls orange.

INSIGHT

Both the sentences above are *negative*. The word *not* makes a sentence negative. (Other words can make a sentence negative also; several are listed on page 106.)

Most negative sentences require helping verbs. In sentence 1, *eat* is the main verb of the sentence and *do* is the helping verb. In sentence 2, _____ is the main verb and _____ is the helping verb. You're correct if you said *inform* is the main verb and *did* is the helping verb.

Most negative sentences require helping verbs.

─────────────── PRACTICE 2 ───────────────

In each of the following negative sentences, underline all parts of the verb. Write *MV* over the main verb and *HV* over any helping verbs. The first one has been done for you.

     HV   MV
1. You <u>should</u> not <u>skip</u> a month with the electric company.

2. They probably will not be quiet without their money.

3. My cousin does not balance his checkbook.

4. I have not been balancing mine either.

5. With a little luck, we will not be in trouble yet.

6. We do not want our wages garnisheed.

Answers start on page 169.

Questions

  1. Are you learning about computers?
  2. When did you enroll in technical school?
  3. Have you been keeping up with the work load?

INSIGHT

Like other sentences, questions require a subject and a verb. However, these are often not as easy to find as they are in statements. Let's take a close look at how to find verbs and subjects in questions.

For each of the three questions, go back and underline all the parts of the verb. Write *MV* over all main verbs and *HV* over the helping verbs. The parts of each verb will not all be next to each other.

Notice that some questions have more than one helping verb. Which question above has two helping verbs? number _____

Check your answers.

Question	Helping Verbs	Main Verbs
1	Are	learning
2	did	enroll
3	Have been	keeping

Now that you have found all of the verbs, it's time to look for the subject of each question. (Remember that the subject is the person or thing that performs the action of the verb.) Circle the subject in each question. Which word is the subject of each question above? _____

You are right if you said the word *you* is the subject of all the above questions. In questions, is the subject *after* or *before* the first helping verb? _____

> **Questions usually have one or more helping verbs.**
> **The subject is after the first helping verb.**

────────────────── PRACTICE 3 ──────────────────

In each question below, write *MV* over the main verb and *HV* over the helping verb or verbs. Then write *S* over the subject. The first one has been done for you.

  1. Where do your classes meet?

  2. How long do the classes last?

  3. Do you have different instructors?

  4. Does your instructor meet with you outside class?

  5. What has the class been working on?

  6. Have you completed part of the work independently?

Answers start on page 170.

Commands

Always work carefully.
Cut the wood slowly in a straight line.
Do not look up at the television.

INSIGHT

The instructions above are in command form. A **command** is a sentence that directly tells someone what to do—or what not to do.

In each command above, underline the verb. In the negative commands, be sure to underline the helping verb as well as the main verb. You should have underlined *work*, *Cut*, and *Do look*.

We have said that every sentence requires a subject. Do you see a subject in the commands above? _____ Commands do *not* contain subjects. That is because the subject is understood to be *you*. *Always work carefully*, means "YOU always work carefully." *Don't lose your temper* means "Don't YOU lose your temper." Because the subject is understood to be *you*, it is not necessary to actually write *you*.

> **In commands, the subject is understood to be *you*.**

——————————————— PRACTICE 4 ———————————————

Some, but not all, of the sentences below are commands. Add the word *you* in parentheses before the verb in each command. If a sentence is not a command, leave the space blank. The first one has been done for you.

1. (You) Ask questions now.

2. _____ The manual explains how to use the saw correctly.

3. _____ Read all of the explanations.

4. _____ Do all of the steps outlined.

5. _____ Safety considerations are the most important.

6. _____ Do not cut corners!

Answers start on page 170.

COMPOUND SUBJECTS, VERBS, AND COMPLEMENTS

Butcher, Baker, Candlestick Maker

Look at the following sentences.

1. The mayor or the city council will brief the reporters on the tax discussion.
2. The council discussed the proposal but voted against it.
3. The council overturned the raises in property taxes, gasoline taxes, and sales taxes.

INSIGHT

As you know, simple sentences follow this form: S-V. (subject-verb). Most sentences also have a complement after the verb.

Each sentence above is a simple sentence. However, each sentence has more than one subject, verb, or complement.

Sentence 1 has two _____ . You're right if you said two subjects. The words *mayor* and *city council* are united by the word *or*.

Sentence 2 has two _____ . You're right if you said two verbs: *discussed* and *voted*, united by the word *but*.

Sentence 3 has three parts to the _____ . You're right if you said three parts to the complement; the words *property taxes*, *gasoline taxes*, and *sales taxes* make up the compound complement. The word *and* unites them.

A simple sentence has a subject and a verb and may have a complement. Each part can be single (one item) or compound (two or more items united by *and*, *or*, or *but*).

> **A *compound subject*, *verb*, or *complement* has
> two or more items united by *and*, *or*, or *but*.**

Picture a simple sentence with compound subjects, verbs, or complements like this:

COMPOUND SUBJECT: The **mayor** or the **city council** will brief the reporters.
COMPOUND VERB: The council **will accept** or **reject** the proposal.
COMPOUND COMPLEMENT: The mayor was **angry** but **articulate**.

——————— PRACTICE 1 ———————

Each sentence contains a compound. Decide if it is a compound subject (CS), compound verb (CV), or compound complement (CC). Write *CS*, *CV*, or *CC* on the line. The first one has been done for you.

__CS__ 1. The mayor and the city council disagreed on the proposal.

_____ 2. The mayor spoke softly but defended the proposal.

_____ 3. The council debated the issue on Monday, Tuesday, and Wednesday.

_____ 4. Councilman Williams and Councilwoman Rossi argued in favor of the tax hike.

_____ 5. Councilman Williams pointed out the advantages for the city's schools, roads, and neighborhoods.

_____ 6. The other council members scorned, rejected, or dismissed the supporters' arguments.

Answers start on page 170.

Using Commas Correctly

You may have noticed that some compounds use commas and others do not. Look at the following examples of compound subjects and try to find the rule for comma use.

1. The mayor and the city council met on Friday.
2. The mayor, the city council, and the governor met on Friday.
3. The mayor, the city council, the governor, and all of their advisers met on Friday.

In sentence 1, how many parts are in the compound subject? _____ In sentence 2? _____ In sentence 3? _____ You're right if you said sentence 1 has two parts, sentence 2 has three, and sentence 3 has four.

Which sentences use commas in the compound subject? Sentences __ and __

Use *no* comma when there are only _____ parts in a compound subject. Use commas when there are _____ or more parts in a compound subject. These rules apply to any compound— subject, verb, or complement.

Notice that when commas are used, they occur *before* the word *and*, *or*, or *but*—never after.

INCORRECT: The mayor, the city treasurer, or the corporation counsel, will research the proposal.

CORRECT: The mayor, the city treasurer, or the corporation counsel will research the proposal.

Also, do not put a comma *before* the compound items.

INCORRECT: The story is being discussed by, reporters, photographers, and editors.
CORRECT: The story is being discussed by reporters, photographers, and editors.

Use commas when the compound has three or more items.
Remember: *1 and 2* but *1, 2, and 3*.

Don't forget to use the word *and, or,* or *but* in a compound. At the same time, be careful not to overuse these words.

> AWKWARD: Schools, roads, public works need funding.
> AWKWARD: Schools and roads and public works need funding.
> SMOOTH: Schools, roads, and public works need funding.

─────────────── PRACTICE 2 ───────────────

Add commas where they are needed. Some sentences do not need any commas. The first one has been done for you.

1. Tax hikes are brought up, discussed, and often rejected.

2. State and city governments often need more money for schools roads or other projects.

3. Mayors or governors frequently ask and fight for higher taxes.

4. Candidates representatives and the public generally oppose increased taxes.

5. Sales taxes are naturally unpopular with merchants and customers.

6. Some people write letters form committees or use their votes against higher taxes.

7. Others accept tax hikes as the only solution to some state and local problems.

─────────────── PRACTICE 3 ───────────────

Combine the sentences to make a new sentence with a compound subject, verb, or complement. To join the sentences, use the word in parentheses. Use commas correctly. The first one has been done for you.

1. More money is needed for schools. More money is needed for roads. More money is needed for public transportation. (*and*) More money is needed for schools, roads, and public transportation.

2. The schools need better facilities. The schools need new buildings. The schools need special programs. (*and*)

3. The buses are expensive. The buses break down frequently. (*but*)

4. The roads are narrow. The roads are bumpy. The roads are full of potholes. (*and*)

5. Taxes can pay for roadwork. Tolls can pay for roadwork. Parking fines can pay for roadwork. (*or*)

6. Community leaders must find solutions to these problems. Lawmakers must find solutions to these problems. (*or*)

———————————— PROOFREAD ————————————

You are an assistant to Brett Harper, the No-Tax party candidate for mayor. You must correct the errors in the following pamphlet before it is printed. Your job is to correct the following mistakes:

● Add or cross out commas when necessary.
● Add or cross out the word *and* or *or* when necessary.

Use an arrow ∧ to show where you are adding something. Sometimes it may be necessary to cross out one thing and add something else in its place. The first error has been corrected for you.

        Brett Harper will be your mayor ∧*and* your no-tax advocate. Brett will

lower taxes, and put our city back together. Here is Brett's plan for

improving conditions in your schools your neighborhoods your homes and

your streets. Brett proposes a volunteer system in the local elementary, and

high schools. Parents, local business people will help students with English

and science and history and math in free after-school programs. Brett

proposes a workfare program for improvement in neighborhoods, and

homes. People can work for their money by repairing local streets, painting

houses, picking up garbage. Brett proposes a crackdown on fines for

parking, and moving violations. Increased fine collection will pay for repairs

in roads, and freeways. Vote for Brett Harper! Brett will get rid of high

taxes, and get our city back in shape!

Answers start on page 170.

AVOIDING FRAGMENTS

Not Saying Enough

Remember that a simple sentence must contain a complete idea and must have a subject and a verb. With this in mind, take a look at the "sentence" in **boldface** that appears in the paragraph below.

> Owning a dog has many important benefits. **First, companionship.** Also, dogs can protect their owners and their property from unwelcome intruders. Finally, dogs can be trained to do many important tasks.

INSIGHT

What is the problem here? Let's see if the example in **boldface** meets the requirements of a simple sentence. Circle the answers.

1. Does it have a verb?		YES	NO	MAYBE
2. Does it have a subject?		YES	NO	MAYBE
3. Does it contain a complete idea?		YES	NO	MAYBE
4. Is this a complete sentence?		YES	NO	MAYBE

You are absolutely right if you said that this was not a complete sentence.

1. There is no verb.
2. Without a verb, there's no way to know if the word *companionship* is a subject or not.
3. There is definitely no complete idea. What is the writer trying to tell us *about* companionship?

Instead of a complete sentence, this is a *fragment*. A fragment is only a part of a sentence, not a whole one. Fragments are confusing to your reader. Complete sentences, on the other hand, transmit your ideas clearly to the reader.

Write complete sentences, not fragments.

─────────────── **PRACTICE 1** ───────────────

Decide if each item below is a complete sentence or a fragment. Write *SENT* for sentence and *FRAG* for fragment. Check each item for the following parts of a complete sentence:

- subject
- verb
- complete idea

Don't go by length alone. It's possible to have a short sentence or a long fragment.

_____ 1. For example, recuperation from an illness.

_____ 2. For example, dogs can help their owners in the recuperation from an illness.

_____ 3. Dogs need special care.

_____ 4. Affection from their owners.

_____ 5. Also, loyal devotion and faithfulness.

_____ 6. In addition, they provide their owners with a sense of security.

_____ 7. Both small and large dogs require.

_____ 8. The necessity of love, care, and proper grooming.

Answers start on page 170.

How to Fix Fragments

Fragments are fairly easy to spot when they stand alone. It is sometimes harder to find them in a paragraph or passage. Below is the beginning of a paragraph. It contains two fragments.

> **(1)** Dogs are the favorite pets of millions of North Americans. **(2)** They provide several benefits for their owners. **(3)** First, companionship. **(4)** Dogs help lonely people. **(5)** Feel loved and needed. **(6)** Dogs are especially good companions for the elderly.

Which are the two fragments? __ and __ Underline them. If you underlined *(3) First, companionship* and *(5) Feel loved and needed*, you were right. Now, how can you fix problems like these?

Sometimes you can just attach a fragment to the sentence before or after it. For instance, *(5) Feel loved and needed* can be attached to *(4) Dogs help lonely people* to create a new, complete sentence. Write that sentence here:

_____

Other types of fragments need more work. For instance, *(3) First, companionship* cannot be attached to anything. Instead, you need to add words to make it a complete sentence. Here are two examples:

> First, **dogs provide** companionship.
> First, companionship **from dogs is important to many people.**

> **There are two ways to fix a fragment:**
> • **Attach it to the sentence before or after it to make one complete sentence.**
> • **Add additional words to make the fragment a complete sentence.**

─────────── **PRACTICE 2** ───────────

Find the fragments below. Then fix the problem by adding each fragment to the sentence before or the sentence after. Think about the meaning! The first one has been done for you.

1. Security is also important. Dogs provide. A sense of safety to residents of high-crime areas.

   Security is also important. Dogs provide a sense of
   safety to residents of high-crime areas.

2. Dogs bark. And alert their owners to danger. Even small dogs can protect their owners.

3. Unfortunately, they can sometimes disturb neighbors. And even family members. Continuous barking can be a real annoyance.

4. Some people are afraid of dogs. A bad experience with one dog. Can be enough to turn some people against all dogs.

―――――――――――――――――――― PRACTICE 3 ――――――――――――――――――――

Rewrite each fragment by adding words to make a complete sentence. Be sure to use words that fit the meaning of the short passage. There may be more than one way to write the new sentence. The first one has been done for you.

1. Dogs can be hard to keep. First, the expense.

   Dogs can be hard to keep. First, the expense may be too much for people on tight budgets.

2. Dogs bring different benefits to their owners. For one thing, protection.

3. Some relatively small breeds make excellent watchdogs. The bull terrier.

4. Security. Another benefit is warm and unquestioning affection.

5. Dogs can be highly affectionate. Wag their tails and give their owners sloppy kisses.

6. Dogs are not for everyone. The lack of freedom for the owner.

―――――――――――――――――――― PROOFREAD ――――――――――――――――――――

As an employee of *Dogs R Us* magazine, you have to edit the following article on dogs. Find and correct fragments:

● Attach them to the sentence before or after, **or**
● Add words to make the sentences complete.

There are eleven fragments in all, and the first one has been corrected for you.

Dogs and people have been friends ~~.~~ ~~For~~ *for* hundreds of years. Some benefits of dog ownership are familiar. To everyone. Others may be less familiar. First, protection. Dogs can use their loud barks or their sharp bites to ward off aggressors. Also, companionship. Dogs keep lonely people company. And give them unquestioning love. Third, better health. Studies have shown that dog owners recover more quickly. From heart attacks and strokes. Than nonowners. Finally, help with work or daily living. For hundreds of years, sheepdogs. Have helped farmers by herding their sheep. All in all, dogs make excellent protectors, companions, and helpers.

Answers start on page 170.

AVOIDING RUN-ONS

Saying Too Much

Read the following paragraph out loud. Remember: Do not pause until you see a period.

> I have four reasons why I am late for this appointment the first one is that my baby wouldn't eat his spinach I had to mash some bananas for him being in a hurry, I threw the banana peels out the window the mailman slipped and fell on one of them he hurt his wrist I had to drive him to the emergency room a policeman pulled me over for speeding the mailman got angry at the policeman and tried to hit him with his good arm then I had to go back home and get some money to get the mailman out of jail I am very sorry that I am late and that I littered.

INSIGHT

Did you have trouble reading the paragraph out loud? By the time you got to the end, you may have run out of breath. Now go back and read the paragraph silently. Was it easy or hard to follow? _____ Why do you think this paragraph was so hard to read out loud and so hard to follow?

If you noticed that there aren't enough periods, you are correct. A period is needed to tell the reader when each sentence ends. Without periods, the reader gets confused and can't tell where one sentence starts and another ends. This makes the ideas seem jumbled and unclear.

Two or more sentences run together are called a **_run-on sentence_**. The paragraph above is one long run-on sentence.

> **Avoid writing run-ons.**

Finding and Fixing Run-ons

Most run-ons are shorter than one paragraph. Here is a common example of a shorter run-on:

> My baby won't eat spinach he'll only eat mashed bananas.

How can you tell that this is a run-on? There are two ways. One way is to read out loud and use your instincts. You can often *hear* the run-on. When your voice wants to go down and pause, there should usually be a period. If there isn't one, it's likely to be a run-on.

A more foolproof way is to check the sentence structure. Remember that a simple sentence has this structure:

| SUBJECT-VERB. | OR | SUBJECT-VERB-COMPLEMENT. |

Compare the structure of a sentence and a run-on:

CORRECT SENTENCES: | S-V. S-V. |

RUN-ON: | S-V S-V. |

The simplest way to correct a run-on is to add a period in the correct place to divide the run-on into separate sentences. Of course, you'll also need to add a capital letter to the beginning of the second sentence.

Go back to the run-on example on page 28 and put the period and capital letter in the right places. It should look like this:

My baby won't eat spinach. He'll only eat mashed bananas.

The following example is also a run-on:

The mailman was in pain, he wanted to get to the hospital right away.

Simply putting a comma between two complete thoughts does not get rid of the run-on.

**The easiest way to correct a run-on is to add a period
and a capital letter in the correct place.**

PRACTICE 1

Look at each group of words and decide if it is a correct sentence or a run-on. (You may want to label subjects, verbs, and complements to help you decide.) Then write *SENT* or *RUN-ON* on the line. The first one has been done for you.

sent 1. I mashed the bananas and threw the peels out the window.

_____ 2. The mailman was in a hurry, he didn't watch where he was going.

_____ 3. I drove to the hospital quickly but carefully.

_____ 4. The policeman spotted me, he said I was going ten miles over the speed limit.

_____ 5. He took my driver's license and gave me a ticket.

_____ 6. The mailman was in pain, he began to yell and tried to hit the policeman.

_____ 7. The policeman easily grabbed his arm then he arrested him.

_____ 8. The mailman knew the policeman, he had run off with the mailman's wife many years ago.

PRACTICE 2

Check your answers to Practice 1. Now rewrite each of the run-ons you found, using periods and capital letters to divide them into separate sentences. Write the corrected sentences on a separate sheet of paper.

Answers start on page 171.

CUMULATIVE REVIEW

Show What You Know

As you work on this exercise, keep in mind everything you've learned about writing good sentences and expressing your ideas clearly to your reader.

When you write correct, complete sentences, your writing will sound both sophisticated and clear. Fragments and run-ons sound clumsy and confuse the reader. Take some time now to review what you've learned about writing correct sentences and avoiding run-ons and fragments.

————————————— PROOFREAD —————————————

Find and correct the fragments and run-ons in the passage below. There are fifteen fragments and run-ons in all, and the first one has been corrected for you.

Major league football and baseball ~~Are~~ *are* very different. All the baseball teams own minor league teams, young players go there to acquire their skills. However, National Football League teams. Draft players right out of college. These players play for the pros right away there are no lower-level teams. For those with less talent.

Professional baseball players. Have longer careers. Their jobs are less dangerous, they do not have as much physical contact as football players do. Many professional football players have bad knees. And need surgery. Furthermore, neck and back injuries.

The average career on a major league baseball team lasts for five years. There is a lot of competition for jobs. Also, deteriorate. A pitcher's control can go, another player's batting average can plummet. It's very risky. No one can guess. About the duration of a young player's career.

Answers start on page 171.

————————— WRITING ASSIGNMENT —————————

It's time now to try putting some of the concepts you've been learning to work—by writing a paragraph on your own. First let's go over what a paragraph is.

A *paragraph* is a group of sentences about a common idea. A paragraph always contains a *topic sentence* that tells the reader what the main idea of the paragraph is. Often the first sentence of a paragraph is the topic sentence. The rest of the sentences in the paragraph support or tell more about the main idea. Sentences that do not fit the main idea do not belong in the paragraph.

Take a look at the example paragraph below. The topic sentence is in **boldface**.

> **People can prevent heart disease in several ways**. First, they should get adequate exercise. Second, they need to follow a low-cholesterol diet. Third, they should not smoke. Finally, they should get regular checkups. If people follow these four guidelines, they have a good chance at a healthy heart.

Notice that the writer has *indented* the first line of the paragraph. That is, the writer started writing a little way in from the margin. This signals the beginning of a new paragraph to the reader and makes the writing easy to follow.

Now it's your turn to write. Choose *one* of the following topics. Then write a paragraph of eight to ten sentences on this topic.

1. Describe three reasons to avoid drinking too much.

2. Describe three ways to stay healthy.

3. Describe three problems in your community.

4. Describe your three favorite stores.

Whichever topic you choose, you should follow these guidelines:

☑ Explain your ideas as clearly and fully as possible.
☑ Write correct, complete sentences.
☑ Try to include a few compound subjects, verbs, or complements.
☑ Avoid fragments and run-ons.

When you are finished, proofread your paragraph carefully to make sure you have written complete sentences and there are no run-ons or fragments.

CHAPTER 2
CONNECTING SENTENCES

Goals

- To combine simple sentences to form compound or complex sentences
- To learn how to punctuate compound and complex sentences
- To understand the meaning of common coordinating and subordinating conjunctions and transition words
- To learn how to use a semicolon to combine sentences
- To recognize and fix different types of fragments and run-ons

COMPOUND SENTENCES

I Can, and I Will

1. My parents sent us to school, and we studied hard.
2. We got good grades, but we never finished school.

INSIGHT

The sentences above are both correct, but they are different from the kinds of sentences you've already studied. Label the subjects and verbs in each sentence with *S*, and *V*. You will need *two* sets for each sentence!

Your labeling should look like this:

        S   V   S   V
1. My parents sent us to school, **and** we studied hard.

       S V   S   V
2. We got good grades, **but** we never finished school.

Neither of these sentences is a run-on. Why not?

In sentence 1, which word connects the two sets of S-V? _____ In sentence 2, which word connects the two sets of S-V? _____ What punctuation is used before the words *and* and *but*? _____ You're right if you said a comma.

Sentences 1 and 2 are *compound sentences*. A compound sentence is simply two complete sentences connected by *coordinating conjunctions*, or joining words, such as *and* and *but*. A comma is used before the coordinating conjunctions.

You can picture a compound sentence as the sum of two separate sentences:

> My parents sent us to school.
> + We studied hard.
> _____
> My parents sent us to school, **and** we studied hard.

Good writers often combine simple sentences into compound sentences to make their writing sound smoother and more sophisticated. A paragraph or longer piece of writing with just simple sentences will seem choppy and clumsy to a reader. That's why it's important to be comfortable using a variety of sentence types.

> **In a compound sentence, two complete sentences
> are joined by a comma and a coordinating conjunction.**

Remember that the words *and* and *but* do not have the same meaning. They cannot be used interchangeably. The word *and* means that the second part of the sentence is *adding* something to the first. The word *but* means that the second part of the sentence will be talking about something that contrasts with the first part:

> Our parents were proud of our grades, **but** they couldn't let us stay in
> school.

—————————— PRACTICE 1 ——————————

Combine the following pairs of sentences with a comma and the correct coordinating conjunction: *and* or *but*. Remember that only the first letter of a sentence should have a capital letter. The first one has been done for you.

1. We got good grades. We couldn't finish school.
   We got good grades, but we couldn't finish school.

2. My parents worked in the fields. I worked with them.

3. We worked long hours every day. We didn't make much money.

4. We didn't earn much. The bills kept piling up.

5. My brothers kept their jobs. I quit.

6. They wanted security. I wanted better pay.

7. There were more jobs up north. I wanted one.

Answers start on page 171.

Other Coordinating Conjunctions

Word	Meaning	Example
so	shows the result of a situation	I couldn't earn enough money, **so** I looked for another job. (Looking for a new job was the *result* of not earning enough money.)
or	shows a choice	I needed a new job, **or** I would never get anywhere in life. (The *choice* was between getting a new job or going nowhere.)
yet	shows something opposite or unexpected	The field work was low paying, **yet** my brothers kept their jobs. (The brothers kept their jobs even though the work was low paying.)
for	shows the reason for a situation	My brothers stayed on the farm, **for** they felt secure there. (The *reason* why the brothers kept their jobs was because they felt secure.)

Now look at punctuation. As you saw on page 33, in all compound sentences a comma is used before the coordinating conjunction. Study the structure of a compound sentence:

S-V, _____ S-V.
and
but
so
or
yet
for

Joining Three or More Sentences

It is possible to have a compound sentence that joins three (or even more) complete sentences. Look at the examples below.

1. I went to Detroit, and my brothers stayed in Mississippi.
2. I went to Detroit, my brothers stayed in Mississippi, and my sister moved to Atlanta.

In sentence 2, three complete sentences are joined. Notice that the coordinating conjunction (*and*) is used only once—before the last sentence. A comma is used after each sentence before the coordinating conjunction.

> **A compound sentence that joins three or more sentences takes this form:**
>
> S-V, S-V, _____ S-V.

──────────── PRACTICE 2 ────────────

Combine the following sentences with the correct coordinating conjunction. Sometimes more than one is possible. Don't forget to use commas. The first one has been done for you.

1. I loved my home. I had to leave.

   I loved my home, but I had to leave.

2. I needed to find a new job. My family wouldn't make it.

3. There were more jobs up north. I moved to Detroit.

4. I found a job in an auto factory. My income rose significantly.

5. The job paid extremely well. I took it.

6. I was earning good money. I still wanted to return to school.

7. I went back to school. I didn't quit my new job.

8. I worked days. My wife worked nights. Her mother watched the children on Saturdays.

Answers start on page 171.

──────────── PRACTICE 3 ────────────

Complete these compound sentences, using the coordinating conjunctions provided. Make sure that the meaning makes sense. Also make sure that the part *you* add has a subject, a verb, and a complete idea. The first one has been done for you.

1. I wanted to get my GED, but . . .

   I wanted to get my GED, but I needed to earn money.

2. The community center had classes available during the daytime, and . . .

3. My boss refused to cut my hours, so . . .

4. I could either quit my job, or . . .

5. My spouse wanted me to continue my education, for . . .

6. We wanted to earn a lot of money right away, yet . . .

Answers will vary.

CONNECTING IDEAS

On the Other Hand

1. Lucilla works in a fast-food restaurant. She never eats any of her meals there.
2. Lucilla works in a fast-food restaurant. **However,** she never eats any of her meals there.
3. Lucilla works in a fast-food restaurant; **however,** she never eats any of her meals there.

INSIGHT

In line 1 there are two separate, simple sentences. They are both grammatically correct, but if you read them together, they sound choppy.

In line 2, the word *However* has been added to the beginning of the second sentence. The word *However* is called a **transition**. This word makes the two sentences read a little more smoothly and shows a relationship between them. On the one hand, Lucilla works in a fast-food restaurant, yet, surprisingly, she never eats there.

There are many other words or phrases that can connect the ideas in different sentences. Below is a list of some of the more common ones along with their meanings.

Time Order

First,	Second,	Third,	Last,	Next,	Then
After . . . ,	Before . . . ,	At that time,	During that time,	Finally	

First, heat the milk until it is warm but not boiling. **Second,** slowly stir in the melted chocolate.

Rosa's kitchen filled with smoke as her pot roast burned. **After that disaster,** she and her guests went out dancing.

Additional Ideas

First,	Second,	Third,	In addition,	Also,
Finally,	Last,	Furthermore,	Moreover,	

I think you should get a job. **Furthermore,** I think you should start paying your mother rent.

I don't like those plaid pants. **In addition,** your cologne smells terrible.

Specific Examples

For example,   For instance,   To illustrate,

You don't always let me know what's going on. **For example,** you could have called yesterday about this afternoon's meeting.

Summing Up
In summary,   In conclusion,   In short,   All in all,   On the whole,

Clark is handsome, intelligent, charming, and kind. **In short,** I really like him.

Contrast
The words and phrases below show that one idea is in contrast to—is in opposition to—another idea.
However,   On the other hand,   Nevertheless,   In contrast,

Marguerite wants to stay out late every night. **However,** her mother wants her to come home at ten.

Marguerite likes to have fun. **On the other hand,** she wants to do well in school.

Effects
These words and phrases show the *result* of something.
Therefore,   For this reason,   Consequently,   As a result,

Hans didn't wake up until noon today. **Therefore,** he didn't get to work until one o'clock.

Hans missed an entire morning of work. **For this reason,** his boss was very angry.

What punctuation do you see right after most of the words and phrases in **boldface** above?

a _____ You're right if you said a comma.

———————————— PRACTICE 1 ————————————

Copy and complete each sentence. Make sure your answers make sense. The first one has been done for you.

1. Whirlpool baths are expensive to install. For this reason, . . .

   Whirlpool baths are expensive to install. For this reason, not many people own them.

2. Black-and-white television was once considered a miracle of technology. Then . . .

3. Small cars are less expensive than big cars. In addition, . . .

4. Many appliances that were revolutionary a few years ago are now obsolete. For example, . . .

5. VCRs are coming down in price. As a result, . . .

6. A microwave oven can save cooking time. On the other hand, . . .

7. Compact discs provide crystal clear sound and don't get scratched or worn easily. Consequently, . . .

8. Technology is advancing at an increasingly rapid rate. However, . . .

Answers will vary.

—————————————— **PRACTICE 2** ——————————————

In the passage below, fill in the appropriate word or phrase. Choose a transition word or phrase from pages 36–37. Make sure the one you use makes sense. Remember to add a comma after it. The first one has been done for you.

Hector works on Helpline. Helpline is a telephone hotline that provides two main services. ___First,___ it gives callers the chance to discuss
<u>1</u>
their problems with trained volunteer counselors. _____ it
<u>2</u>
gives referrals to professionals or agencies that can help the callers further.

In his Helpline work, Hector is able to help people who are depressed or upset. In several cases, he has been able to prevent a suicide.

_____ Hector finds this work very satisfying.
<u>3</u>

_____ at times Hector finds his work frustrating. When he
<u>4</u>
hangs up the phone, he cannot know if the callers will take steps to help themselves. _____ Hector knows at least that he has been a
<u>5</u>
sympathetic listener and that the callers do not feel so alone with their

problems. _____ Hector is very glad that he became a Helpline
<u>6</u>
volunteer.

Answers start on page 172.

Using Semicolons Correctly

Now take another look at sentences 2 and 3 from the example on page 36:

2. Lucilla works in a fast-food restaurant. **However,** she never eats any of her meals there.
3. Lucilla works in a fast-food restaurant**; however,** she never eats any of her meals there.

In sentence 3, circle the punctuation mark that appears before the word *however*. This mark $\boxed{;}$ is called a *semicolon*. It is used to combine the two sentences into one. Notice that a comma still follows the word *however*, which links the ideas. As mentioned earlier in this lesson, a comma always appears after a transition that links sentences.

INCORRECT: Lucilla loves french fries; on the other hand the smell of grease makes her sick.

CORRECT: Lucilla loves french fries; on the other hand, the smell of grease makes her sick.

Remember also that a comma *cannot* be used in place of a semicolon.

INCORRECT: She wants to keep her skin clear, therefore, she eats mostly fruit and vegetables.

CORRECT: She wants to keep her skin clear; therefore, she eats mostly fruit and vegetables.

Occasionally a semicolon can be used to join two sentences where there is no transition at the beginning of the second sentence. In these cases the two sentences must have a clear relationship to each other. It is not correct to link two unrelated sentences with a semicolon.

> INCORRECT: Lucilla wants to get a new job; Francisco was on the phone for five hours Friday night.
> CORRECT: Lucilla wants to get a new job; she would like to get out of the fast-food business.

A semicolon [;] can be used to join two sentences.
The correct form is

S-V; (*transition*), S-V.   or   S-V; S-V.

—————————————— **PRACTICE 3** ——————————————

Rewrite the sentences correctly in two ways: once with a period and once with a semicolon. Use capital and small letters correctly. Remember to add commas where needed. The first one has been done for you.

1. The restaurant where Lucilla works is very busy for example it sells over 500 hot dogs on an average day.

   The restaurant where Lucilla works is very busy. For
   example, it sells over 500 hot dogs on an average day.
   The restaurant where Lucilla works is very busy; for
   example, it sells over 500 hot dogs on an average day.

2. The building is shaped like a giant hot dog as a result the inside is very long and narrow.

3. It is hard to move around the employees bump into each other constantly.

4. The owner refuses to air condition the building therefore the employees who cook get very hot.

5. Lucilla doesn't have to cook on the other hand she does have to serve hot and surly customers.

6. Lucilla is tired of looking at all those hot dogs furthermore she dreams about them every night.

Answers start on page 172.

Alternate Placement of Transitions

A transition can appear in the middle of a sentence as well as at the beginning. When a transition is placed in the middle of a sentence, it is surrounded by commas.

> Hector had to man the phones by himself last night.
> **In addition,** there were several crank calls. OR
> There were, **in addition,** several crank calls.

What is wrong with the sentences below?

> Hector had had a rough night last night. He decided; **therefore,** to treat himself to a hot dog for lunch today.

The problem here is that the word *therefore* is not joining together two complete ideas. It is simply an interrupting word in the second sentence. See what happens if we split apart the two parts of the sentence:

> He decided.
> Therefore, to treat himself to a hot dog for lunch today.

Do these two lines make sense as separate sentences? No! In fact, the second line is a fragment with no subject and no verb. In this instance, the word *therefore*, just like the other transitions listed on pages 36–37, should simply be set off by commas:

> He decided, **therefore,** to treat himself to a hot dog for lunch today.

―――――――――――――――― PRACTICE 4 ――――――――――――――――

Some of these sentences are punctuated correctly, and some are punctuated incorrectly. Cross out the incorrect punctuation and add the correct comma or semicolon where necessary. If the sentence is correct as written, write *OK* in the blank. The first one has been done for you.

_____ 1. Hector saw an attractive woman working behind the counter; consequently, he decided to talk to her.

_____ 2. She seemed bored with her job. She was; however, eager to talk to him.

_____ 3. Hector told her about his rough night at Helpline; next, he mentioned that they needed volunteers.

_____ 4. Lucilla was quite interested, for example, she asked him what kind of training volunteers received.

_____ 5. She had been looking for another job. She felt; on the other hand, that volunteer work might also make her life more meaningful.

Answers start on page 172.

COMPOUND ELEMENTS VERSUS COMPOUND SENTENCES

I Came, I Saw, I Conquered

1. Cassius plowed the west field.
2. Cassius plowed the west field and came home at noon for lunch.
3. Cassius plowed the west field, so he was ready to begin planting.

INSIGHT

Only one of these sentences is a compound sentence: $\boxed{\text{S-V, \_\_\_\_ S-V.}}$ The other two are simple sentences.

Which one is a compound sentence? ____ You're right if you chose sentence 3. Only sentence 3 has two sets of subjects and verbs joined by a coordinating conjunction.

       S   V   S   V
Cassius plowed the west field, **so** he was ready to begin planting.

Sentence 1, as you know, is a simple sentence with one subject and one verb. Sentence 2 is also a simple sentence. Why? Sentence 2 has two verbs (*plowed* and *came*), but how many subjects does it have? _____

You're right if you said one: *Cassius*. Sentence 2 is *not* a compound sentence because a compound sentence must have at least two sets of S-V joined by a coordinating conjunction.

A compound sentence *must* look like this: $\boxed{\text{S-V, \_\_\_\_ S-V.}}$
A sentence that does not have this structure is *not* a compound sentence.

Here are examples of different types of sentences.

Simple sentence

   S   V
Cassius finished his work at sundown.

Simple sentence (*with compound S, V, or C*)

   S   S   V
Cassius and Lucius finally cleared the land.
   S   V   V
Cassius plowed the west field and added fertilizer.
   S   V   C   C
Cassius planted corn and potatoes.

Compound sentence

   S   V   S   V
Cassius plowed the west field, so he was ready to begin planting.

─────────────── **PRACTICE** ───────────────

Write *SS* for simple sentence or *CS* for compound sentence. Remember that a compound sentence must have at least *two* sets of S-V. The first one has been done for you.

_SS_   **1.** We had a serious and demanding instructor in Detroit.

──────   **2.** We submitted our papers, and the instructor gave a new assignment immediately.

──────   **3.** The assignments were unusually long and difficult.

──────   **4.** One assignment was short and easy, but the students grumbled about it.

──────   **5.** The holiday weekend was coming, several students were leaving town, and no one wanted to think about homework.

──────   **6.** The instructor was sympathetic, yet he left the assignment on the board.

──────   **7.** After all, he was going to spend *his* holiday with a mountain of exams.

──────   **8.** Finally, he gave in and erased the assignment from the board.

──────   **9.** Later, we learned some interesting news about our instructor's holiday weekend.

──────   **10.** He had left his exams in his desk, locked his office door, and taken a bus to Atlantic City.

Answers start on page 172.

Using Commas Correctly

Which sentences below need commas and why? Add commas and then check your answers.

    1. I worked very hard and my bank account grew quickly.
    2. I worked very hard and saved my money.

Sentence 1 is a compound *sentence*. It has two sets of S-V. A comma is needed before the conjunction *and*.

Sentence 2 is a simple sentence with a compound *verb*. Both verbs (*worked* and *saved*) have the same subject (*I*). No comma is needed between the two verbs. (If sentence 2 had had three or more verbs, a comma would be needed to separate the three items.)

> **Remember how to use a comma in a compound sentence:**
>
> | S-V, ____ S-V. |

———————— **PROOFREAD** ————————

You are sponsoring a Youth Work Program, and you have asked a leading community member to write her success story. You hope it will inspire the young people in your program. Unfortunately, the comma key was not working on her typewriter.

YOUR JOB: Add commas where they belong. Five commas need to be added.

I did not grow up in a wealthy family. My mother worked hard and barely made the monthly bills. We always had enough to eat but dinners included a lot of rice and beans. My sister and I slept in the living room and studied at the kitchen table. My mother always encouraged us in our studies and she checked our homework every night. My high school teachers also encouraged me so I applied for a college scholarship. College was not easy but I worked hard. I graduated and was hired by the National Insurance Company. I am now an account manager there. Hard work contributed to my success but so did encouragement from my family and teachers.

Answers start on page 172.

COMPLEX SENTENCES

Superiority Complex

1. When Laura tried out for the play.
2. The director was thrilled.
3. The director was thrilled when Laura tried out for the play.

INSIGHT

Which group of words above is a fragment? _____ You're right if you chose line 1. It does not contain a complete idea—what *about* when Laura tried out for the play? Line 1 is also called a *clause* because it has a subject and a verb (*Laura* and *tried*); however, this clause is not a sentence. Not every clause is a complete sentence.

> **A clause is a group of words that contains a subject and a verb.**

Line 2 is a simple sentence, the type you studied in Chapter 1. It has a subject (*director*) and a verb (*was*), and it tells a complete idea.

Now take a look at line 3, which is also a correct, complete sentence. It has been formed by combining lines 1 and 2. Underline the part of the sentence formed by line 2. Now circle the part formed by line 1. Your work should look like this:

The director was thrilled (when Laura tried out for the play.)

The underlined part of the sentence is called the *main clause*. It could stand alone as a separate sentence. The circled part is known as a *dependent clause*—that is, it *depends* on the main clause to make a complete sentence. A dependent clause cannot stand alone as a separate sentence. You saw this when you looked at line 1—even though the clause had a subject and a verb, it did not tell a complete idea.

A sentence with a main clause and a dependent clause is called a *complex sentence*. In a complex sentence, the dependent clause can go either before or after the main clause. Compare these sentences:

The director was thrilled when Laura tried out for the play.
When Laura tried out for the play, the director was thrilled.

In the examples above, underline the main clause in each, and circle the dependent clause.

> **A main clause can stand alone, but a dependent clause cannot.**
> **A dependent clause and a main clause together make up a complex sentence.**
> **In a complex sentence, the dependent clause can go before or after the main clause.**

─────────────────── PRACTICE 1 ───────────────────

Underline each main clause, and circle the dependent clause.

1. When Laura tried out for *West Side Story*, the director was thrilled.

2. Because the leading lady had quit, the director needed a new actress for the part of Maria.

3. Laura read the part after three other actresses had tried out.

4. The director wanted Laura for the part as soon as he heard her.

5. Although the others were more experienced, Laura had the right touch.

6. While the others could read lines more smoothly, Laura captured the spirit of Maria more vividly.

Answers start on page 172.

Subordinating Conjunctions and Commas

Different words and phrases can begin a dependent clause. Go back to Practice 1 and underline those words. Write them here: _____, _____, _____, ___ _____ ___, _____, _____. Conjunctions that begin dependent clauses are called *subordinating conjunctions*. The subordinating conjunctions in Practice 1 are only a few examples. You will learn other such joining words soon.

Let's concentrate on punctuation now. Go back to Practice 1 and circle all of the commas. You should have circled commas in sentences 1, 2, 5, and 6. Why do these sentences have commas but not sentences 3 and 4? In sentences 1, 2, 5, and 6, is the dependent clause first or second? _____

> **When the dependent clause is first, use a comma after it.**
> **When the main clause is first, do not use a comma.**
>
> _____ S-V, S-V.   or   S-V _____ S-V.

─────────────────── PRACTICE 2 ───────────────────

Circle the subordinating conjunction in each sentence. Then add any necessary commas. (Not every sentence needs a comma!) The first one has been done for you.

1. (When) Laura came home from her audition, her family wanted to know everything.

2. Although she didn't know for sure she was hoping for the role of Maria.

3. Her family still had more questions after she had told them everything.

4. Before she had a chance to answer them the phone rang.

5. The director called because he had some good news.

6. As soon as Laura hung up she jumped for joy.

———————————— PRACTICE 3 ————————————

Rewrite each sentence by changing the order of the main and dependent clauses. Add or remove commas as necessary. The first one has been done for you.

1. She had never been in a play before she got the part in *West Side Story*.

   <u>Before she got the part in West Side Story, she had</u>
   <u>never been in a play.</u>

2. Because she had once studied acting, she had some preparation.

3. She began to study her lines as soon as she got the script.

4. When the director criticized her reading, she felt upset.

5. She felt better because she saw her own improvement.

6. Before the curtain went up, she was terrified.

7. She remembered all her lines even though she was nervous.

8. The audience went wild when the curtain went down.

Answers start on page 173.

SUBORDINATING CONJUNCTIONS

Because I Said So

There are different kinds of subordinating conjunctions that can be used in dependent clauses. Below is a list of some of the more commonly used subordinating conjunctions, grouped according to their meanings.

Time	Examples
before after when while until as soon as by the time	**When** the alarm rang, the workers looked up. The alarm rang twice **while** they were working.

Conditions	Examples
if unless whether as long as	We will go on the picnic **unless** it rains. **Whether** it rains or not, I want to go.

Cause and Effect	Examples
since because so that	**Since** money is tight, I can't go to the movies. I need to save money **so that** I can pay all my bills.

Contrast	Examples
although even though even if while	**Although** he was wealthy, he was not happy. I'll be fine **even if** you leave me. **While** Tom is rich, his sister is poor.

──────────── PRACTICE 1 ────────────

Complete each sentence by adding a main clause. Pay careful attention to the meaning of the sentence. Add commas where they are needed. The first one has been done for you.

1. Before I go to work . . .

 <u>Before I go to work, I eat a big breakfast.</u>

2. . . . if I arrive late.

3. Before I go to sleep . . .

4. . . . when I wake up in the morning.

5. While I am at work . . .

6. . . . as soon as I get home.

7. Unless I have a good reason . . .

Answers will vary.

──────────── PRACTICE 2 ────────────

This exercise gives you special practice with the contrast words, which can be tricky.

● Combine a clause on the left with the correct clause on the right.
● Use one of these contrast words: *although, even though, even if,* or *while.*
● Write each sentence two ways. In the first sentence, put the main clause at the beginning. In the second sentence, put the main clause at the end. Reread your work to make sure all your sentences make sense.

The first one has been done for you.

1. we must believe in ourselves

 they may be difficult

2. we must try our hardest

 it may hurt our pride

3. we must finish our studies

 we may feel like giving up

4. we must put up with criticism from disloyal friends

 our friends don't believe in us

<u>We must believe in ourselves even if our friends don't believe in us.</u>
<u>Even if our friends don't believe in us, we must believe in ourselves.</u>

Answers start on page 173.

──────────── PRACTICE 3 ────────────

Copy and complete each sentence by finishing the dependent clause in a logical way. The first one has been done for you.

1. Although . . . , it is still worth the money.

 <u>Although college is expensive, it is still worth the money.</u>

2. Although . . . , I still want to keep at it.

3. While I sometimes get discouraged, . . .

4. . . . even though that is not likely.

5. . . . even if some of my friends disagree.

Answers will vary.

MORE WITH FRAGMENTS

Pieces of a Complex Whole

Which of the following is a correct sentence?

1. He practices the saxophone often.
2. Because he practices the saxophone often.

INSIGHT

You're right if you saw that line 1 is correct; it has a complete idea. Line 2 is not a complete sentence. (Do you find you want to ask, "*What happens* because he practices his saxophone so often?") Write the word that is in line 2 but not line 1: _____.

Because is a subordinating conjunction, and it signals the beginning of a dependent clause. As you know from your work in this chapter, a dependent clause must be attached to a main clause—it cannot stand alone. In fact, a dependent clause standing alone is a fragment—something to avoid at all costs.

The fragment can be fixed by adding a main clause to go with the dependent clause:

Because he practices the saxophone often, **Alvin has become an accomplished musician**.
Alvin's teachers consider him a model music student because he practices the saxophone often.

A dependent clause alone is a fragment, not a sentence.

—————————————— PRACTICE ——————————————

Find the sentences and the fragments. Look for dependent clauses on their own. Write *SENT* or *FRAG*. The first one has been done for you.

Frag **1.** When Alvin finishes music school.

_____ **2.** He will be proud.

_____ **3.** Because he will soon graduate from music school.

_____ **4.** Surprisingly, some people are not so pleased.

_____ **5.** Even though his family is proud.

_____ **6.** Although his family is proud, his friend Ron is jealous.

_____ **7.** Because Ron dropped out of music school and never returned.

_____ **8.** Ron doesn't want Alvin to succeed either.

_____ **9.** Alvin tries to ignore his friend when Ron criticizes him.

_____ **10.** He has made new friends at school.

_____ **11.** While he played in the jazz ensemble.

_____ **12.** Right now, he just feels happy because he is about to meet his first goal.

————————————— **PROOFREAD** —————————————

You are a new instructor in a GED program. One of your students has written a moving essay, and you want to submit it to the local newspaper for publication.

YOUR JOB: Correct the errors in the complex sentences. Fix the fragments and add or cross out commas as necessary. The first error has been corrected for you.

When I was sixteen years old, I dropped out of school. I wasn't learning anything. Because I had lost interest. Although a few teachers reached out to me. Some did not even pay attention to me in class. Because I wanted to belong somewhere. I joined a gang. Of course, I completely lost interest in school, after I became a gang member. While life on the streets was tough I couldn't imagine a different life and certainly didn't believe in any future. Then I got shot in a fight. While I was in the hospital. I had a lot of time to think. I had a choice between death in the streets and the chance for a new life in school. When I was eighteen years old I enrolled in GED courses. Although sometimes I want to quit. I will try to make it this time.

Answers start on page 173.

MORE WITH RUN-ONS

Making Compound Fractures

Refresh your memory. What is wrong with the words below?

Personal stereos transmit good sound, they shut out other noise.

What is the problem? The words do not make up a single sentence. Instead, we have a _____. You are right if you said that that is a run-on. You have learned one way to fix run-ons: add a p_____ and a c_____ letter in the correct places. Rewrite the run-on above as two sentences:

_____

You should have put a period after the word *sound* and a capital *T* in the word *they*. In this section, you are going to be learning other ways to fix run-ons.

Using Coordinating Conjunctions

People can listen to loud music on personal stereos, others around them won't be bothered by the noise.

INSIGHT

This run-on could be fixed by making it into two sentences, *or* it could be made into a compound sentence using a coordinating conjunction (*and, but, yet, so, or, for*).

People can listen to loud music on personal stereos, **yet** others around them won't be bothered by the noise.

> **To fix a run-on, you can make it into a compound sentence by adding a coordinating conjunction.**
> **Remember to add a comma before the coordinating conjunction.**

PRACTICE 1
Fix these run-ons by adding a coordinating conjunction (*and, but, yet, so, or, for*). Add a comma if necessary. The first one has been done for you.

1. Personal stereos have earphones, the sound enters the ear directly.
   Personal stereos have earphones, so the sound enters the ear directly.

2. The sound drowns out other noises, listeners can tune out their surroundings.

3. Some people use personal stereos on the bus they may use them at work.

4. Many people like to cover up outside sounds others find this distracting.

5. Personal stereos transmit sound only to the listener other people are not bothered by the noise.

6. Personal stereos offer many advantages they have at least one disadvantage.

Answers start on page 173.

Using Subordinating Conjunctions

Here is another run-on:

> Portable radios have powerful sound systems some people call them boom boxes.

INSIGHT

You now know two ways to fix run-ons. (1) You could add a period and a capital letter to make two sentences, or (2) you could add a coordinating conjunction and a comma to make a compound sentence. Rewrite the run-on both ways.

1. _____

2. _____

Check your answers. They should look like this:

1. Portable radios have powerful sound systems. **Some** people call them boom boxes.
2. Portable radios have powerful sound systems, **so** some people call them boom boxes.

There is still another way to fix the run-on—by making it into a complex sentence with a subordinating conjunction:

> **Because** portable radios have powerful sound systems, some people call them boom boxes.

You can also add a subordinating conjunction in the middle of a sentence, as in this example:

> RUN-ON: Portable radios can be taken anywhere they are battery powered.
> SENTENCE: Portable radios can be taken anywhere **since** they are battery powered.

> **To fix a run-on, you can make it into a complex sentence**
> **using a subordinating conjunction (*before, while, because*, etc.).**
> **Remember to add or remove commas where necessary.**

─────────────────── PRACTICE 2 ───────────────────

Fix the following sentences by using one of these subordinating conjunctions: *because, although, even though, when.* Use commas correctly. The subordinating conjunction could go at the beginning or the middle of the sentence, depending on the meaning. The first one has been done for you.

1. Her neighbors blast their radio, Karen can't concentrate.

When her neighbors blast their radio, Karen can't concentrate.

2. Some people love loud music, it can disturb others.

3. Some people get angry others don't respect their need for quiet.

4. A few people like portable radios the noise can keep other people away.

5. Some people play their music in a public place, they feel protected.

6. Portable radios are prohibited on buses in many cities, some people play them anyway.

Answers start on page 174.

Run-on Review

You have learned three ways to fix a run-on:

1. Make it into two separate sentences by adding a period and a capital letter.
2. Make it into a compound sentence by adding a coordinating conjunction (*and, but, so, yet, for, or*).
3. Make it into a complex sentence by adding a subordinating conjunction (*because, when,* etc.).

——————————— PROOFREAD ———————————

You are a maintenance engineer at Shady Towers, a large apartment complex. The landlord, your employer, has recently posted a letter to all residents. Partly because the letter is so poorly written, the tenants have disregarded it completely.

YOUR JOB: Find and correct the run-ons using the three techniques you have studied. There are eight errors in all. The first one has been corrected for you.

We at Shady Towers want all our tenants to be satisfied, ⁀so we are presenting these rules:

1. Tenants should notify the management they plan to have a party.

2. In their apartments, tenants should turn off all radios and stereos after 10:30 P.M. on weekdays they should turn them off by midnight on weekends.

3. Tenants must dispose of garbage properly incinerators should be used for this purpose.

4. Tenants may install air conditioners, these air conditioners must be approved by the management.

5. Tenants may not use kerosene space heaters, these violate fire laws.

6. Tenants may use barbecue grills in the patio area they may not bring the grills inside this also violates fire laws.

Answers start on page 174.

REVIEW

Compound and Complex Sentences

Compare the following sentences:

1. Many people have remote control devices to change channels. They can ignore commercials.
2. Many people have remote control devices to change channels, **so** they can ignore commercials.
3. Many people can ignore commercials **because** they have remote control devices to change channels.
4. Many people have remote control devices to change channels; **therefore,** they can ignore commercials.

INSIGHT

All of these sentences mean the same thing: having remote control devices allows people to ignore TV commercials. Sentences 2, 3, and 4 show three different ways the ideas can be combined into one sentence.

In sentence 2, the word _____ combines the ideas. *So* is a coordinating conjunction, and a comma goes before it to join the sentences together.

In sentence 3, the word _____ combines the ideas. *Because* is a subordinating conjunction that begins a dependent clause, so no comma is needed before it. If the dependent clause is moved to the beginning of the sentence, a comma follows the dependent clause:

> **Because** many people have remote control devices to change channels, they can ignore commercials.

In sentence 4, the word _____ combines the ideas. *Therefore* is a transition. A semicolon goes before this word and a comma follows it. A period could also be used instead of a semicolon so that the word *therefore* starts a new sentence.

> Many people have remote control devices to change channels. **Therefore,** they can ignore commercials.

It's important to keep in mind which kind of word you are using to join sentences because each requires different punctuation. The word and phrase lists on pages 34, 36–37, and 47 can be a reference guide when you are in doubt.

———————————— PRACTICE ————————————

Read each pair of sentences. Rewrite the pair using the joining word or phrase given. Remember to punctuate correctly. The first one has been done for you.

1. Commercials are supposed to attract attention.
   Many are ignored at first. (*while*)

   While commercials are supposed to attract attention, many are ignored at first.

2. Commercials are supposed to attract attention.
   Many are ignored at first. (*but*)

3. Commercials are supposed to attract attention.
   Many are ignored at first. (*however*)

4. Most commercials are repeated frequently.
   People notice them eventually. (*as a result*)

5. Most commercials are repeated frequently.
   People notice them eventually. (*so*)

6. Most commercials are repeated frequently.
   People notice them eventually. (*because*)

7. People claim to ignore commercials.
   They are often influenced by them. (*although*)

8. People claim to ignore commercials.
   They are often influenced by them. (*but*)

9. People claim to ignore commercials.
   They are often influenced by them. (*nevertheless*)

Answers start on page 174.

CUMULATIVE REVIEW

Show What You Know

In this section, you have learned how to write good simple, compound, and complex sentences. At the same time, you have learned to avoid writing run-ons and fragments. Pull together all you know as you do the next activities.

——————————— PROOFREAD ———————————

The tenants at Shady Towers apartment complex have drafted a letter of complaint to the management.

YOUR JOB: Correct the fragments and run-ons. There are fifteen errors in all, and the first one has been corrected for you.

To the Management:

We, the tenants of Shady Towers, are dissatisfied~~y With~~ *with* the

maintenance of our apartments. And the public areas of the building.

When the temperature dropped below freezing last winter. The radiators

were not functioning as a result, the apartments were intolerably cold. The

pipes froze, they burst, several apartments were flooded. The management

has not paid for the damage to the furniture. Or the carpeting and curtains.

Furthermore, the hallways. The doors to the incinerators are stuck on

several floors, the tenants must leave their garbage in the halls there is

nowhere else to put it.

Finally, the lobby. The locks on the outer doors are broken, hoodlums

can get in and loiter by the elevators. Two tenants have been threatened

they are now afraid to go in or out of the building.

The conditions of this building are dangerous and unlivable, we have

consulted with a lawyer. And with the Tenants' Rights Organization. We are

prepared to take a series of legal steps, however we will call them off. If the

management remedies the above-mentioned problems.

Sincerely,

The Tenants of Shady Towers

Answers start on page 174.

———————————— WRITING ASSIGNMENT ————————————

You have a complaint, and you wish to write a letter to the proper authority. Write three paragraphs of about six to eight sentences each. Choose one of the following:

1. You are dissatisfied with the conditions of your apartment or rented house. Write a letter to the building management describing your complaints in full.

2. You are dissatisfied with the facilities and conditions of your child's school. Write a letter to the school principal describing your complaints in full.

3. You are dissatisfied with the conditions of your community as a whole. Write a letter to your representative in the local government describing your complaints in full.

Naturally, you wish the receiver of your letter to give it serious and respectful attention. For this reason, you must write a letter that is both sophisticated and grammatically correct. To accomplish this, do the following:

☑ Include a *variety* of sentence types (simple, compound, and complex).
☑ Use correct coordinating conjunctions and subordinating conjunctions to make your ideas clear. Make sure you are using them correctly.
☑ Make sure all your sentences are complete and that you are not writing fragments or run-ons.

When you are finished, proofread your work to make sure you have done all the above correctly.

CHAPTER 3
SENTENCE BUILDING BLOCKS

Goals

- To understand what a noun is and how to use various types of nouns: proper and common, regular and irregular plural, possessive, and noncount
- To understand how to use various types of pronouns: subject, object, possessive, and reflexive
- To understand what adjectives and adverbs are and when to use each

---

NOUNS

People, Places, Things, and Ideas

What do *all* the following words have in common?

1. man woman child politician driver
2. city country park street field
3. book telephone rock water sand
4. love happiness anger security problem

INSIGHT

All of the words above are called **nouns**. To learn what a noun is, circle the answers to these questions.

Each of the words in line 1 above is a(n) . . .
person place thing idea

Each of the words in line 2 is a(n) . . .
person place thing idea

Each of the words in line 3 is a(n) . . .
person place thing idea

Each of the words in line 4 is a(n) . . .
person place thing idea

A noun is a word that represents a person, place, thing, or idea.

━━━━━━━━━━━━━━━ **PRACTICE 1** ━━━━━━━━━━━━━━━

Circle the nouns in each sentence.

1. My office is a pleasant place.

2. The furniture is comfortable, and the carpet is new.

3. There are pictures on every wall, and there are several large windows.

4. The workers and the boss share the same room.

5. Therefore, communication between management and employees is easy.

6. There are many meetings but few arguments.

7. Of course, some problems exist, but this situation is much better than my former job.

Answers start on page 174.

Proper Nouns

A noun that names a specific person, place, or thing is called a ***proper noun***. Below is a list comparing common nouns and proper nouns:

Common	**Proper**
woman	Elizabeth King
school	Roberto Clemente High School
minister	Reverend Holbrook
cat	Pinkface
street	Cahuenga Boulevard

The proper nouns all begin with a _____ letter. You're right if you said a *capital* letter.

As you write, you may wonder when you should be capitalizing some nouns. Remember that only nouns that are someone or something's *name* need to be capitalized. If the noun can stand for many different people or things, it is a common noun.

> Doctor Canty has written a book on skin care.
> A doctor wrote *A Healthy Complexion for the Rest of Your Life*.

Is the following sentence correct?

> My Doctor says I eat too much salt.

No! The word *doctor* should not be capitalized. The word *my* tells us that the writer means one specific doctor, but the writer has not actually *named* the doctor.

─────────── **PRACTICE 2** ───────────

Some of the sentences below are correct as written, some need proper nouns to be capitalized, and some have common nouns incorrectly capitalized. Cross out those nouns and write the correct words above them. If the sentence is correct as written, write *OK* in the blank. The first one has been done for you.

_____ 1. The management feels that the ~~international bricklayers union~~ *International Bricklayers Union* should be prepared to make some concessions.

_____ 2. When the Bruneldi family was in trouble, a bankruptcy judge was able to help.

_____ 3. A court-supervised repayment plan is almost always preferable to filing for bankruptcy, judge Macklin has written.

_____ 4. My Psychiatrist wants me to take a personality test.

_____ 5. According to Doctor Greenwood, this test will reveal much about my Unconscious Thoughts.

_____ 6. The newspaper had a story this morning about noise levels in the sports stadium.

_____ 7. My Mother dislikes all of my friends.

_____ 8. According to Mom, they are all irresponsible bums.

Answers start on page 175.

SINGULAR AND PLURAL NOUNS

One Potato, Two Potatoes

Nouns can be *singular* (*one tin soldier*) or *plural* (*two tin soldiers*). To make a singular noun plural, most of the time just add the letter *s* to the noun.

one newspaper   two newspaper**s**
a fact   many fact**s**
an opinion   several opinion**s**

To make most nouns plural, simply add *s* to the singular noun.

When you write the plural form of a noun, add the letter *s* only—*do not* add an apostrophe ⬚.

WRONG: many idea's
RIGHT: many ideas

Sometimes the spelling changes when the letter *s* is added to a noun. Here are two important rules to remember:

1. Add *es* to words ending in *s, z, sh, ch,* and *x* (boss—boss**es**).
2. If the letter *y* appears after a consonant, change *y* to *i* and add *es* (secretary—secretari**es**.) If the *y* appears after a vowel, do not change it (key—key**s**).

For more information on spelling plurals, look at Contemporary's *Edge on English: All Spelled Out Book C.*

──────────── PRACTICE ────────────

Write the plural form of these nouns.

1. a manager—two _____

2. one worker—seven _____

3. an employee—a hundred _____

4. one box—twenty _____

5. a typewriter—several _____

6. a copy—a number of _____

7. one machine—two _____

8. an idea—many _____

Answers start on page 175.

Irregular Plurals

There are some plural forms that are *irregular plurals*—that is, they do not follow the *s* spelling rules. A good dictionary will give you the spelling of all irregular plurals. The following are some common ones:

Plurals ending in *oes*
Add *es* to the following words that end in the letter *o*:
    potato—potato<u>es</u>   tomato—tomato<u>es</u>   echo—echo<u>es</u>   hero—hero<u>es</u>   veto—veto<u>es</u>

Plurals ending in *ves*
In the following words, change the singular endings *f* and *fe* to *ves*:
    shelf—shel<u>ves</u>   wife—wi<u>ves</u>   half—hal<u>ves</u>   life—li<u>ves</u>   loaf—loa<u>ves</u>
    knife—kni<u>ves</u>   leaf—lea<u>ves</u>

Plurals that do not change form
These animal names use the same form in the singular and plural:
    fish—fish   sheep—sheep   deer—deer

Common irregular plurals
These plurals do not take the letter *s*:
    man—m<u>en</u>   woman—wom<u>en</u>   child—child<u>ren</u>   person—pe<u>ople</u>   foot—f<u>ee</u>t
    tooth—t<u>ee</u>th   mouse—mi<u>ce</u>

Other irregular plurals
    crisis—cris<u>es</u>   basis—bas<u>es</u>   hypothesis—hypothes<u>es</u>   criterion—criteri<u>a</u>

———————————————— PROOFREAD ————————————————

You are editing a book about different social service careers. This short piece appears in the book.

YOUR JOB: Correct the irregular plurals. There are eleven errors in all, and the first one has been done for you.

Some social service agencies give free help to ~~peoples~~ *people* who have

suffered financial and emotional crisies. They may help families by finding

them food, shelter, and clothing. They may work with husbands and wifes

who have had violent arguments. They may work with childrens whose lifes

have been disrupted by abuse. Mens, womens, and their childrens must

meet several criterias to receive free help. They must show a need for help

and a lack of ability to pay for it. Peoples who work for these agencies do

not achieve fame, but they are considered heros by some of their clients.

Answers start on page 175.

POSSESSIVE NOUNS

Workers' Compensation

On page 61, you learned *not* to use an apostrophe when you are making a plural. In this lesson, we will look at situations where an apostrophe *is* required. Look at the example sentence:

> The employee's uniform is green.

INSIGHT

In the sentence above, what is green—the employee or his uniform? _____ You are right if you said *uniform*. Obviously, the uniform is green, not the employee!

Whose uniform are we talking about? the _____'__

Employee's is a **possessive noun**, a noun that shows ownership. That is, the sentence is saying, "The uniform of the employee is green." The *'s* is what makes the noun a possessive. Now look at this example:

> The employees' cafeteria was closed.

Is the cafeteria for one or more than one employee? _____ You're correct if you said *more than one*. The cafeteria is for a group of employees. What is used to indicate that *employees'* is a possessive? __ You're correct if you said that just an apostrophe is added to the end of the plural.

As you know, some irregular plural nouns do not end in the letter *s*. To make these nouns possessive, add *'s*.

> The **people's** clothing is green.
> The **children's** clothing is green.

Singular Possessive	**Plural Possessive**	**Irregular Plural Possessive**
Add *'s*: the employee's job	Add ⬚ : the employees' jobs	Add *'s*: the people's jobs

—————————— PRACTICE ——————————

In the sentences below, the **boldface** nouns are supposed to be possessive.

- Add an apostrophe alone ⬚ to make a regular plural noun possessive.
- Add an apostrophe and the letter *s* (*'s*) to make a singular noun or an irregular plural noun possessive.

The first one has been done for you.

1. The **employees'** work has been excellent. Promote them.

2. The **employee** work has been excellent. Promote her.

3. This is the **managers** opinion. Listen to them.

4. This is the **president** opinion. Listen to her.

5. The **company** profits have increased. It is a successful business.

6. The **companies** profits have been very high. These companies have used new methods of production.

7. The **people** reactions have been very positive.

8. The **women** raises have been the same as the **men** raises.

Answers start on page 175.

Apostrophe or Not?

Does an apostrophe belong in the word in **boldface** below?

The workers' opinions were different from the **managers'**.

Yes! Here it's understood that *the managers'* means *the managers' opinions.* To check your writing, always add the understood noun in your mind. That is, you can write *the managers',* but you should check yourself by mentally saying *the managers' opinions.*

Does an apostrophe belong in the **boldface** word below?

The **manager's** made a decision.

No! A noun needs an apostrophe *only* when it is possessive. Do not add an apostrophe to a plural noun that is not possessive.

WRONG: The **manager's** made a decision.
  RIGHT: The **managers** made a decision.
        (Here *managers* is the subject of the sentence and doesn't possess
        anything.)
  RIGHT: The **managers' decision** will affect all the workers.
        (Here *decision* is the subject, and *managers'* tells whose decision it
        was.)

——————————— PROOFREAD ———————————

A friend has written a paragraph to present to his daughter's social studies class, which is studying the world of work. He wants to make sure the paragraph is clear and easy for the students to follow.

YOUR JOB: Add apostrophes to the paragraph only where they are necessary. There are five apostrophes in all that need to be added, and the first one has been done for you.

I belong to a union. My union's policies protect the workers in my

industry. When a workers rights are violated, he can speak to his

representatives. To deal with the grievance, the unions representatives then

speak with the companys. The union also protects workers as a whole. Of

course, some unions have serious problems. There is a lot of corruption in

some unions leadership.

Answers start on page 175.

COUNT/NONCOUNT NOUNS

Diamonds and Rust

You have learned about singular and plural nouns. Now let's look at a different kind of noun.

one dollar—two dollars—a hundred dollars—money

INSIGHT

You can count dollars. *Dollar* can be singular (one dollar), or plural (two dollars or a hundred dollars). On the other hand, you cannot count the word *money*. To be sure, try it:

one money?—two moneys??—a hundred moneys???

Nouns like *dollar* are called **count nouns** because they can be counted. Count nouns can be either singular or plural. Nouns like *money* are called **noncount nouns** because they cannot be counted. They never have a plural form. Look at some more examples of count and noncount nouns, then see if you can add to the list:

Count Nouns	Noncount Nouns
dollar(s)	money
cup(s)	water
slice(s)	bacon
party(ies)	fun
_____	_____
_____	_____

> **If you can't count it, it's a noncount noun.**
> **Noncount nouns do not have a plural form.**

―――――――――――――― PRACTICE 1 ――――――――――――――

Write the plural form of all count nouns. (Watch out for irregular plurals.) If the noun is noncount and has no plural form, write *X* in the blank. The first two have been done for you.

1. bracelet _bracelets_
2. jewelry ___X___
3. furniture _____
4. chair _____
5. problem _____

6. anger _____
7. rice _____
8. dish _____
9. child _____
10. honesty _____

Answers start on page 175.

Expressions Used with Count and Noncount Nouns

How many (*money/dollars*) do you have left?
How much (*money/dollars*) do you have left?

If you said *How many dollars* and *How much money*, you were correct. The word *many* is used with a count noun like *dollars*. The word *much* is used with a noncount noun like *money*.

Sometimes writers get confused about which expressions go with plural count nouns and which go with noncount nouns. Study the list below. Say them out loud with a sample noncount noun (such as *water*) and a sample count noun (such as *cups*). Notice that some expressions are the same in both columns.

Noncount	Count (Plural)
how much	how many
much	many
a lot of	a lot of
some	some
a little	a few/several
more	more
most	most
less	fewer
an amount of/ a great deal of	a number of
this/that	these/those

───────── PRACTICE 2 ─────────

Write the correct expression for each noun. The first one has been done for you.

1. How ___much___ water was on the floor? (*much/many*)

2. Only _____ raindrops came through the front window. (*a little/a few*)

3. Even _____ rain came through the back window. (*less/fewer*)

4. How _____ paper towels did you use up? (*much/many*)

5. I used only _____ towels. (*a few/a little*)

6. How _____ time did you spend on the cleanup? (*much/many*)

7. I spent _____ minutes on the cleanup. (*several/much*)

8. You had _____ problems with the storm than we did. (*less/fewer*)

9. _____ storms are always hard on the windows. (*These/That*)

10. _____ of glass gets broken by the hail. (*A great deal/A number*)

11. We always have to replace _____ of windows. (*an amount/a number*)

12. _____ weather can change every five minutes. (*This/These*)

Answers start on page 175.

PRONOUNS

You and Me, Babe

I like my doctor.
She tries to be open and honest when she talks to patients.

The word *She* refers to a word in the first sentence. Which word does it refer to? *my* _____

You are right if you said *doctor*. What kind of word is *doctor*—a noun or a verb? _____

You are right again if you said that *doctor* is a noun. The word *she* is not a noun. It is a **pronoun**. A pronoun is a word that stands in place of a noun. Notice another pronoun above. The word *I* is also a pronoun—it is how you refer to yourself, and it stands in place of your own name.

> **A pronoun is a word that stands in place of a noun.**

Subjects and Objects

A pronoun can be the subject of a sentence, as in this example:

They helped the lab technician yesterday.

INSIGHT

Here the people (*they*) are performing the action—they are giving the help.

A pronoun can also be the *object* of a sentence:

The lab technician helped **them** this morning.

In this case, the people (*them*) are *receiving* the help, not giving it. While a subject performs the action of a sentence, an object receives it.

Before continuing with pronouns, let's spend some time understanding *objects*.

> **An object *receives* the action of the verb. It can be a noun or a pronoun.**

The chief of nursing called everyone together.
The chief of nursing spoke to the night-shift nurses.

In the first sentence, the object (*everyone*) directly follows the verb (*called*). In the second sentence, the object (*night-shift nurses*) follows a preposition (*to*). A **preposition** is a small word that shows the relationship between a noun or pronoun and the rest of the sentence.

Here is a list of common prepositions:

with	for	about	under	above
to	by	in	over	around
from	of	on	at	near

Objects can follow verbs or prepositions.

──────────── PRACTICE 1 ────────────

Each subject and each object is in **boldface**. Label each with *S* or *O*. Remember: a subject performs the action of the verb, and an object receives the action. The first one has been done for you.

1. **The doctor** told **Stan** what the test results were.

2. **She** showed **the data** that led her to diagnose diabetes.

3. **He** asked many **questions** about the disease.

4. After an hour, **Stan** understood **the precautions** he would need to take to stay healthy.

5. **The doctor** reassured **him** that he could live a normal life.

6. Next **Stan** met with **the nurse**.

7. **She** showed **him** how to give himself insulin shots.

8. **He** also learned about **blood sugar levels** and how to measure them.

9. **Stan** promised **himself** to be very careful in his eating habits.

10. **He** made **an appointment** to come back in six weeks.

Answers start on page 175.

Subject and Object Pronouns

You now know the difference between a subject and an object. Now look at these sentences:

1. **I** helped the lab technician yesterday.
2. The lab technician helped **me** this morning.

INSIGHT

Why are there two different pronouns even though we're talking about the same person? The word *I* is the _____ of its sentence, and the word *me* is the _____ of its sentence. You are right if you saw that *I* is a subject and *me* is an object.

> **Different pronouns are used for subjects and objects.**

Subject Pronouns	Object Pronouns
I*	me
you	you
he	him
she	her
it	it
we	us
they	them

*The word *I* is the only pronoun that always uses a capital letter.

PRACTICE 2

Circle the correct pronoun. The first one has been done for you.

1. My doctor helps (*I*/**me**) when I have difficulties with my diabetes.

2. Because (*he*/*him*) is diabetic himself, (*he*/*him*) is very helpful and patient.

3. (*I*/*Me*) trust (*he*/*him*) as much as I can trust any physician.

4. The other members of my diabetes support group generally agree with (*I*/*me*).

5. (*They*/*Them*) didn't like our old doctor, however.

6. (*I*/*Me*) agreed with (*they*/*them*) about this person.

7. Our old doctor was high-strung and impatient, and (*she*/*her*) was not sympathetic to (*we*/*us*).

8. As a result, (*we*/*us*) had little respect for (*she*/*her*).

9. Much to our relief, (*she*/*her*) left her practice last month to go into research.

10. Our new doctor is one of (*we*/*us*).

Answers start on page 175.

Pronouns in Compound Subjects and Objects

1. Mr. Kim and _____ saw the doctor yesterday.
2. The doctor saw Mr. Kim and _____ yesterday.

INSIGHT

Add the pronouns *I* and *me* to the sentences above. Be careful!

If you added *I* to sentence 1 and *me* to sentence 2, you are absolutely correct. Notice that the subject of sentence 1 is a compound subject: *Mr. Kim and I.* The object of sentence 2 is also a compound: *Mr. Kim and me.*

It is easy to make a mistake with a compound. To avoid problems, just focus on the pronoun part of the sentence:

. . . _____ saw the doctor. (*I* or *Me?*)
Mr. Kim and **I** saw the doctor.

The doctor saw . . . _____. (*I* or *me?*)
The doctor saw Mr. Kim and **me**.

———————————— PRACTICE 3 ————————————

Write your own sentences with the following compounds. Be careful to use the compounds correctly as subjects or objects. The first two have been done for you.

1. Mr. Kim and I <u>Mr. Kim and I discussed our insurance plans.</u>
2. Mr. Kim and me <u>The nurse spoke to Mr. Kim and me.</u>
3. my coworkers and me
4. my relatives and I
5. they and we
6. them and us
7. you and me
8. you and she
9. him and her
10. his family and he

Answers will vary.

POSSESSIVE PRONOUNS

Not Our Fault

ROBERTO: **My** head is killing me.
AMANDA: So is **mine**!

INSIGHT

The two pronouns in **boldface** are possessive. Roberto is talking about his head, and Amanda is talking about her head. Why is *my* used in one case and *mine* in the other?

Look after each possessive. Do you see a noun after the word *my*? _____ Do you see a noun after the word *mine*? _____ The noun *head* is used after *my*. No noun follows *mine*, however. Here, the noun *head* is understood but not stated.

> **There are two types of possessive pronouns.**
> **One is used before a noun,**
> **and the other is used when there is no noun after it.**

Pronoun + Noun	Pronoun Alone
my head	mine
your head	yours
his head	his
her head	hers
its head	its
our heads	ours
their heads	theirs

IMPORTANT: Do you see any apostrophes in these pronouns? _____ *Never* use an apostrophe in a possessive pronoun!

WRONG: I have my ideas, and she has **her's**.
RIGHT: I have my ideas, and she has **hers**.

——————————— PRACTICE ———————————

Cross out each **boldface** word in the paragraph below and add the correct possessive pronoun. Watch for places where pronouns like *my* and *your* are appropriate. The first one has been done for you.

       Roberto and Amanda had been working at ~~**Roberto and Amanda's**~~ _their_ calculators all day. Unfortunately, **Roberto's** figures were not the same as **Amanda's**. Amanda said, "I have an idea. You check **Amanda's** work, and I'll check **Roberto's**." After twenty minutes, Roberto snapped his fingers and said, "**Amanda's** work is fine, and so is **Roberto's**. The calculators have done **the calculators'** job correctly, too. The problem is **Roberto and Amanda's** boss. He gave one of us the wrong data to work on. Therefore, it was **the boss's** mistake, not **Roberto and Amanda's**." "You're right," said Amanda. "Now, who wants to tell him?"

Answers start on page 176.

FOCUS ON APOSTROPHES

It's My Party

You have just learned that apostrophes should never be used in possessive pronouns (*the house that is **theirs**, **its** roof*). Writers sometimes get confused because some words that *sound* similar to possessive pronouns do use apostrophes. Take a look at these sentences:

You're smart. = You are smart.   It's smart. = It is smart.
They're smart. = They are smart.   He's smart. = He is smart.

INSIGHT

The words *you're*, *they're*, *it's*, and *he's* are not possessives—they are contractions. A **contraction** is the combination of two words into one, using an apostrophe. For example, *you're* is the pronoun *you* plus the verb *are*. The letter *a* of *are* disappears, and an apostrophe appears in its place.

You are smart.
You're smart.

Now compare a possessive pronoun and a contraction:

You're smart. **Your** ideas are interesting.

Look at the words *you're* and *your*. For which one can you substitute the complete form *you are*? _____ Clearly, you can say "You are smart." Can you also say "You are ideas are interesting"? No! That doesn't make any sense.

> **Use an apostrophe in a contraction, not in a possessive pronoun.**
> **To be sure you need an apostrophe,**
> **try substituting the words that the contraction stands for.**
> **If the substitution does not make sense, you have a possessive, not a contraction.**

——— PRACTICE ———

On each line, write the correct word. The first one has been done for you.

Roberto works for an accounting firm. (*He's/His*) __He's__ a diligent
employee, and tomorrow is (*he's/his*) _____ one-year review. Roberto's
boss is planning the points (*he's/his*) _____ going to make. He intends
to say, "Roberto, (*you're/your*) _____ work has been excellent, and
(*you're/your*) _____ a valuable member of our company. I spoke with
two of my superiors about you yesterday. (*They're/Their*) _____
extremely interested in promoting you, and (*they're/their*) _____ word
carries a lot of weight. We are especially pleased with the work you did on
the Miami project and feel that (*it's/its*) _____ success depended in

great part on (*you're/your*) _____ efforts. Therefore, (*it's/its*) _____
                              9   10
my pleasure to inform you that (*you're/your*) _____ going to be pro-
                                                11
moted at the end of this quarter."

Answers start on page 176.

Review

You have learned two situations in which to use apostrophes: in noun possessives and in contractions. To refresh your memory, look at these examples:

> NOUN POSSESSIVE: **Amanda's** boss made an error.
> CONTRACTION: **He's** normally very careful.

You have also learned that apostrophes do *not* belong in possessive pronouns or in nonpossessive plurals.

> POSSESSIVE PRONOUN: **His** boss is the same as **hers**.
> NONPOSSESSIVE PLURAL: Her **efforts** are appreciated.

> **Use apostrophes in noun possessives and contractions.**
> **Do not use apostrophes in possessive pronouns or nonpossessive plurals.**

──────────── PROOFREAD ────────────

You are Amanda's boss. Her one-year review is coming up, and you have written your report for her file. Your assistant has typed it up but has made some mistakes with apostrophe use.

YOUR JOB: Correct the errors in noun possessives, contractions, and possessive pronouns. There are twelve errors in all, and the first one has been done for you.

Amanda Otero has worked in my department for several years now.
Ms. ~~Oteros~~ *Otero's* work has been consistently diligent and reliable. She has

frequently put in extra hours to fulfill the companys needs and has

contributed significantly to it's current healthy state. Shes always

conscientious about checking and correcting her own work. In addition, Ms.

Oteros approach to her work has been innovative. Shes able to analyze

situation's effectively even when their not familiar to her. The result is fresh

solution's to old problems. In fact, I have often reconsidered my own

suggestions after hearing hers. Finally, she gets along well with her

coworkers. She respects they're views and is never afraid to say "Your

right" to someone who points out a problem in her work. All in all, its my

pleasure to recommend a raise.

Answers start on page 176.

REFLEXIVE PRONOUNS

Me, Myself, and I

Don will help **himself**.

INSIGHT

In the sentence above, label the subject and the object with *S* and *O*. Do the subject and the object refer to the same person or to different people? _____ In the sentence above, Don is giving help, but he is also receiving it! You were right if you saw that both the subject and the object refer to the same person.

Notice that the object pronoun here is not *him* but rather *himself*. *Himself* is a **reflexive pronoun**.

A reflexive is used when the object refers to the subject.

Singular	Plural
myself	ourselves
yourself	yourselves
himself	themselves
herself	
itself	

Note: Never write *hisself* or *theirself*. Also, notice that all plural possessives end in *selves*. Never write *ourself* or *themself*. Finally, write *yourself* only when you are referring to one person.

A reflexive can also be added to a sentence to give extra emphasis to the subject or object. Look at these examples:

I **myself** will do the job. (No one else will help but me.)
Ms. Lauten will finish the project **herself**. (She will do it alone.)
I wish to speak to the president **himself**. (I refuse to speak to anyone else.)

A reflexive can be used *with* a subject or object to add emphasis.

─────────────────── PRACTICE ───────────────────

Some of the following sentences, but not all, have errors. Find and correct the mistakes by writing the correct reflexive pronoun. If a sentence has no error, write *OK* in the blank.

_____ **1.** Sometimes I don't understand myself.

_____ **2.** Shawn asked hisself why he had failed at his first job.

_____ **3.** The employees theirselves contributed to their evaluations.

_____ **4.** Dora had no one but herself to blame for her poor review.

_____ **5.** When I was young, my brother said to me, "You yourself must make the decision to do well in school."

_____ **6.** You and your family must take care of yourself if all of you wish to remain healthy.

_____ **7.** The people realized that they had brought disaster upon themself.

_____ **8.** Above all, we must be able to depend on ourself if we want to succeed.

Answers start on page 176.

A Common Problem

What is wrong with this sentence?

The people directed their questions to myself.

Remember that a reflexive pronoun belongs as an object pronoun _only_ when it refers to the subject. In the sentence above, the subject is _people_; clearly, _myself_ does not refer to this word. Instead of the reflexive _myself_, a normal object pronoun (like _me, him, her,_ etc.) should be used. Which pronoun would be correct? _____ Take a look at the correct sentence:

The people directed their questions to **me**.

Now try another problem sentence. What is wrong here?

Hilary and myself will give the presentation.

Here the word _myself_ is acting as part of a compound subject. While a reflexive can be used _with_ a subject to add emphasis, it cannot be the subject itself. To see the problem and the solution, try using _myself_ as the subject alone:

?? **Myself** will give the presentation. ??
I will give the presentation.
Hilary and **I** will give the presentation.

————————————— PROOFREAD —————————————

Your coworker has written a memo and asks you to look it over.

YOUR JOB: Correct the errors in the use of reflexive pronouns. There are five errors in all, and the first one has been corrected for you.

We must work hard to complete the Hastings project by the April deadline. The preparation itself will take several days, so we must allot two full weeks to the entire job. Selena and ~~myself~~ I will do the preparation, but we expect the rest of you to dedicate yourself to the actual writing. William will be the one to present the report. Before his presentation, William must review it hisself. Therefore, all participants must push themself to verify every aspect of the report. If you have any questions, contact Selena or myself.

Answers start on page 176.

ADJECTIVES

The Good, the Bad, and the Ugly

Arizona has a **warm** climate.
Arizona has two **major** cities: Phoenix and Tucson.

INSIGHT

The words in **boldface** are called *adjectives*. To find out the function of an adjective, answer these questions.

What kind of climate does Arizona have? _____

What kind of cities are Phoenix and Tucson? _____

What kind of words are *climate* and *cities*? (circle one)   **a.** nouns   **b.** verbs

You're right if you said the climate is warm and the cities are major. You're right also if you saw that *climate* and *cities* are nouns. The adjectives *warm* and *major* describe the nouns that come after them. You can visualize the sentences like this:

Arizona has a warm climate. It has two major cities.

> **Adjectives are words that describe nouns.**
> **Adjectives can tell what kind, which one, or how many.**

PRACTICE 1

Underline the adjective in each sentence. Underline one word only. Draw an arrow from the adjective to the noun or nouns it describes. The first one has been done for you.

1. Arizona has a warm climate.

2. Phoenix has high temperatures in the summer.

3. Phoenix has pleasant weather during the months of December, January, and February.

4. Phoenix is a popular center for tourists in the winter.

5. Near Phoenix, there are interesting places to visit.

6. Tourists can visit fascinating ruins left by the Hohokam Indians.

7. Visitors are awed by beautiful mountains.

Answers start on page 176.

─────────────── **PRACTICE 2** ───────────────

Think about where you live. Write complete sentences using the words below. Include at least *one* adjective before the noun given. The first three have been done for you.

1. My . . . climate

   ___My state has a harsh climate.___

2. I . . . community

   ___I live in an exciting community.___

3. There . . . museums

   ___There are several interesting museums.___

4. My . . . climate	9. There . . . places to
5. My . . . weather	10. There . . . buildings
6. I . . . community	11. There . . . parks
7. I . . . street	12. There . . . roads
8. There are . . . places	

Answers will vary.

Another Use for Adjectives

The climate is **warm**.

In the sentence above, which word is the adjective? _____ Which word does *warm* describe? _____

Notice that the adjective *warm* describes the subject, *climate*. You have seen that adjectives can appear *before* nouns to describe them. An adjective in the complement can also describe the subject of a sentence.

To see the two ways that adjectives can work, compare the two sentences below. In each sentence, an arrow has been drawn from *warm* to *climate*.

   Arizona has a warm climate.
   The climate is warm.

Often, as in the sentence above, adjectives appear in the complement after the verbs *am, is, are, was, were*, etc. However, adjectives can come after certain other verbs as well. Look at these examples:

   The climate **is** warm.
   The air **feels** dry.
   The sky **looks** clear.

Verbs like these are called *linking verbs* because they *link* the complement to the subject. In each example above, the adjective in the complement is linked to the subject.

Below is a list of common linking verbs. In each example, underline the linking verb and draw an arrow from the adjective back to the subject. One has been done for you as an example.

Linking Verb	Example
act	The woman <u>acted</u> nervous.
appear	The woman appeared afraid.
am, is, are, was, were	She was shaky.
become	She became ill.
feel	She felt dizzy.
grow	She grew calm.
look	She looked relaxed.
seem	She seemed hungry.
smell	The pizza smelled delicious.
sound	It sounded good to her.
taste	It tasted wonderful.

**An adjective can come after a linking verb (LV)
to describe the subject of a sentence:**

S-LV-adjective.

──────────── PRACTICE 3 ────────────

Imagine that you are on a beach. Copy and complete each sentence about your experience there. Use an adjective in the complement after the linking verb. The first one has been done for you.

1. The sky looks . . .

   The sky looks peaceful.

2. The sun feels . . .

3. The air smells . . .

4. The weather looks . . .

5. The wind is . . .

6. The water is . . .

7. The waves are . . .

8. The people on the beach seem . . .

9. The children sound . . .

10. My sandwich tastes . . .

11. I feel . . .

Answers will vary.

ADVERBS

Quickly but Carefully

One baby cried loudly while the other slept peacefully.

INSIGHT

The complex sentence above has two verbs. Write them here: _____ and _____.

Now look at the words that follow each verb. Write them here: _____ and _____.

Words like *loudly* and *peacefully* are called **adverbs**. Like adjectives, adverbs describe other words in the sentence, but adverbs describe action verbs (like *cried* or *slept*).

How did one baby cry? _____ How did the other baby sleep? _____

As you can see, the adverbs *loudly* and *peacefully* tell *how* the babies cried and slept.

> **Adverbs describe action verbs. They answer the question "how?"**

Most adverbs are formed simply by adding *ly* to the end of an adjective. *Loud* and *peaceful* are adjectives. *Loudly* and *peacefully* are adverbs. If an adjective ends in the letter *y*, change *y* to *i* before adding *ly*. Look at these examples:

   loud + ly = loudly   peaceful + ly = peacefully   happy + ly = happily

Here are some common irregular adverbs that do not end in *ly*:

   well   fast   low   hard   right

─────────────── PRACTICE 1 ───────────────

Below is a list of adjectives. Change each one to an adverb. Watch out for irregulars.

1. peaceful _____   **5.** fast _____

2. kind _____   **6.** hard _____

3. quiet _____   **7.** angry _____

4. noisy _____   **8.** good _____

Answers start on page 176.

─────────────── PRACTICE 2 ───────────────

Write ten sentences about yourself, using the adverbs below. The first one has been done for you.

1. badly _I play bridge badly._ _____

2. carefully   7. slowly

3. carelessly   8. sloppily

4. conscientiously   9. well

5. quietly   10. badly

6. fast   **Answers will vary.**

Other Uses of Adverbs

You have learned that adverbs describe action verbs. Adverbs can also describe adjectives and other adverbs. Here are some examples:

John is extremely shy. He speaks extremely quietly.

In the first sentence, the adverb *extremely* describes the adjective *shy*. In the second sentence, the adverb *extremely* describes the adverb *quietly*.

Here are some adverbs that are used frequently to describe adjectives and other adverbs:

extremely   slightly   really
very   quite   somewhat

Do not substitute the adjective *real* for the adverb *really*.

    WRONG: John is **real** handsome.
    RIGHT: John is **really** handsome.

Adverbs can describe verbs, adjectives, or other adverbs.

─────────────── PRACTICE 3 ───────────────

Add one of these adverbs to the sentences below: *extremely, slightly, really, very, quite, somewhat*. The first one has been done for you.

1. John was embarrassed by the situation.
    John was somewhat embarrassed by the situation.

2. John was surprised by his sister's behavior.

3. Dan was rude to the customers.

4. Sadie felt happy about her newest boyfriend.

5. Carol worked hard to meet the deadline.

6. Brenetta spoke confidently to the audience.

7. Sam acted unsure of himself at the meeting.

Answers will vary.

ADJECTIVES VERSUS ADVERBS

Fine or Finely?

What is wrong with this sentence?

He writes neat.

INSIGHT

One word is wrong. Keeping in mind what you have learned about adjectives and adverbs, write the wrong word here: _____. If you wrote *neat*, you were right.

What kind of word is *neat*?   **a.** adjective   **b.** adverb

You are right again if you said that *neat* is an adjective, not an adverb. The problem is that *writes* is an action verb, so an adverb is needed in the sentence. If *neat* is the adjective, what is the adverb? _____

Here is the correct sentence:

He writes **neatly**.

How could the adjective *neat* be used correctly? Recall that adjectives can describe nouns and pronouns and they can come after linking verbs. Here are two correct sentences:

He is a **neat** person. He is **neat**.

Know when to use adjectives and when to use adverbs.

**Adjectives describe nouns and pronouns. They often come after linking verbs.
Adverbs can describe action verbs, adjectives, and other adverbs.**

Now look back for a moment to the list of linking verbs on page 79. Some of the verbs on this list have more than one meaning. When they change meaning, they may become action verbs instead of linking verbs. Compare these sentences:

She looked happy. (*look* = linking verb)
She looked anxiously at the clock. (*look* = an action)

Your dog smells bad. (*smell* = linking verb)
    This sentence describes the odor the dog gives off.
Your dog smells badly. (*smell* = action verb)
    This sentence describes how well the dog's sense of smell is working.

————————————— PRACTICE 1 —————————————

Keeping in mind the rules for using adjectives and adverbs, circle the correct word in each sentence.

1. Charles is a _____ person. (*tidy*/*tidily*)

2. His house is always _____. (*neat*/*neatly*)

3. Charles cleans his house _____. (*thorough*/*thoroughly*)

4. Without a doubt, he is a _____ housekeeper. (*thorough/thoroughly*)

5. Most of his friends agree that Charles is a _____ father. (*good/well*)

6. By all accounts, he is raising his children _____. (*good/well*)

7. He is teaching his children to think _____ about their actions. (*careful/carefully*)

8. Like all good parents, he is _____ proud of his children. (*real/really*)

Answers start on page 177.

─────────────────── PRACTICE 2 ───────────────────

Write ten sentences about yourself. Use the following adjectives and adverbs correctly. The first two have been done for you.

1. cautious *I am a cautious driver.*

2. very *I drive very cautiously.*

3. careful   7. extremely

4. dangerously   8. slightly

5. well   9. intelligent

6. good   10. real

Answers will vary.

─────────────────── PROOFREAD ───────────────────

You are helping your friend prepare for a job interview. Your friend wants to take an honest look at herself, so she has made a list of her strengths and weaknesses. You look over the list.

YOUR JOB: Correct the errors in adjectives and adverbs. There are eleven mistakes in all, and the first one has been corrected for you.

Strengths hard
1. I am a ~~hardly~~ worker.

2. I complete each task thorough.

3. I ask intelligently questions.

4. I am real enthusiastic about my work.

5. I am helpfully to other workers.

6. I get along good with my superiors.

Weaknesses
1. I am excessive concerned with details.

2. I am very seriously, even when others say I should take a situation light.

3. I tend to get angry too easy.

4. I often feel insecurely about how others see me.

Answers start on page 177.

CUMULATIVE REVIEW

Show What You Know

In this chapter, you have learned about various types of words: nouns, pronouns, adjectives, and adverbs. Keep this knowledge in mind as you work on this exercise.

WRITING ASSIGNMENT

Choose one of the following topics. Write a paragraph of about eight sentences.

1. Write a paragraph about how you would like to change yourself and your life. Describe yourself and your life now, and then tell how you would like to be different in the future.

2. Write a paragraph about your current job. Describe what you like and dislike about it. Then tell how your job could be improved.

3. Write a paragraph about a person that you know and admire. Describe the person and tell the reasons you admire him or her.

When you are finished writing, be sure to proofread your paragraph for the following:

☑ Check that all your sentences are complete and that there are no fragments or run-ons.

☑ Check that you have used a *variety* of sentence types: simple, compound, and complex.

☑ Check that you have used nouns, pronouns, adjectives, and adverbs correctly.

CHAPTER 4
VERB TENSES

Goals

- To use past, present, future, present perfect, and past perfect tenses correctly
- To correctly use past, present, and future continuous
- To use the correct tense when writing a paragraph

PRESENT TENSE

Today and Every Day

Textbooks **give** rules, and the dictionary **gives** definitions.

INSIGHT

There are two verbs in the compound sentence above. Write them here: _____ and
_____. The first verb (*give*) uses the **base form**—the shortest, simplest form of the verb.
The second verb (*gives*) uses the **s-form**: the base form plus the letter *s*.

These verbs are both in the **present tense**: they describe things that are true in general. The
present tense also talks about things that happen regularly:

I **buy** a newspaper and **eat** two doughnuts each morning.

The present tense is used for actions that are true in general or that happen regularly.

The chart below shows how to use the base form and the *s*-form.

Subject	Verb	Example
I you we they plural nouns	base	I **drink** lemonade in the summer. English people **drink** lots of tea.
he she it singular nouns	base + *s*	He **drinks** too much soda. The rat **drinks** from puddles.

Contemporary's *Edge on English: All Spelled Out Book C* can give you additional help in spelling the *s*-form of different verbs. The spelling rules for adding *s* to verbs are basically the same as those for adding *s* to nouns.

─────────────── PRACTICE 1 ───────────────

After each subject, write the correct form of the verb in parentheses. The first one has been done for you.

1. (*eat*) I __eat__ two large doughnuts every morning.

2. (*drink*) Rollena _____ two cans of cola every morning.

3. (*miss*) The Willington brothers _____ the 6:30 A.M. train every day.

4. (*feel*) The boss _____ we should come to work better prepared.

5. (*cook*) (*leave*) She _____ a well-balanced meal in her kitchen at 5:30 A.M. before she _____ for work.

6. (*know*) (*like*) I _____ she is doing the right thing, but I _____ to sleep as long as I can.

7. (*wait*) The bus _____ for me if I am late.

8. (*understand*) (*run*) The Willington brothers _____ that their train _____ on an extremely tight schedule.

Answers start on page 177.

Irregular Present Tense Forms

The base verbs *go, do, have,* and *be* have irregular present tense forms.

Subject	Go	Do	Have	Be
I	go	do	have	am
we, you, they, plural nouns	go	do	have	are
he, she, it, singular nouns	goes	does	has	is

CONTRACTIONS

With the verb *be,* you can use *contractions* instead of writing out the complete forms. Take a look at the examples below:

I am   he is   you are   they are
I'm   he's   you're   they're

─────────────── **PRACTICE 2** ───────────────

Circle the correct present tense form in each sentence.

1. Besides their regular full-time jobs, the Willington brothers (*do/does*) a lot of additional work on the side.

2. Eugene Willington (*go/goes*) to art school at night.

3. Frederick Willington (*am/is/are*) a third baseman for a semiprofessional baseball team.

4. I (*am/is/are*) eager to see one of his games.

5. Both brothers (*have/has*) a lot of natural talent.

6. Eugene (*does/do*) a lot of interesting sketches.

7. They (*am/is/are*) uninterested in their jobs as word processors.

Answers start on page 177.

Negatives and Questions

In negative statements and in questions, the present tense uses two helping verbs: *do* and *does.* Look at these examples:

> I **do not need** a car.
> My father **does not have** a car.
> **Do** you **need** one?
> **Does** your mother **have** one?

Notice that the helping verbs *do* and *does* are used with the base form of the main verb.

Subject	Helping Verb	Example
I, you, we, they, plural nouns	do	**Do** you **want** to go to lunch? They **do** not **care** anymore.
he, she, it, singular nouns	does	**Does** she **love** me? That purse **does** not **match** those shoes.

Instead of writing the complete negative forms *do not* and *does not*, you can use contractions: *don't* and *doesn't*.

do not   does not
don't   doesn't

The exceptions to the rules you have studied above are the words *am, is*, and *are*. These words do not require any helping verbs for negatives or questions.

> I **am not** a crook.
> **Are** you a boy or a girl?

You can also form contractions of *is not* and *are not*:

is not   are not
isn't   aren't

─────────────── PRACTICE 3 ───────────────

A bank officer is asking a man questions about a loan he has applied for. Complete the questions correctly. The first one has been done for you.

1. Q: Where ___do you work ?___

   A: I work for the Johnson Company.

2. Q: Where _____

   A: My wife works for Cindy's Fast Food Restaurants, Inc.

3. Q: How much money _____

   A: I earn $20,000 per year.

4. Q: How much money _____

   A: She also earns $20,000 per year.

5. Q: Why _____

   A: We want the loan because my wife needs a car.

6. Q: Why _____

   A: She needs it to drive to her job. The corporate office just moved to a town twenty miles away.

7. Q: _____

   A: No, we are not in debt to any other bank.

Answers start on page 177.

PAST TENSE

It Was All Over

The president's adviser **testified** last week.
Most people **believed** his words, but some **doubted** them.

INSIGHT

Do the sentences above refer to the present or the past? _____ Which two words are a clue about when the action took place? _____ You're right if you saw that the words *last week* indicate the past. Something else indicates the past: the *ed* endings on the three verbs: *testified, believed,* and *doubted.* These verbs are all in the **past tense**.

> **The past tense describes actions that happened in the past.**
> **Most verbs use the *ed* ending to show the past tense.**
> **The past tense form is the same for all subjects.**

——————————— PRACTICE 1 ———————————

Add *ed* to each verb to change it to the past tense.

1. (*appear*) The president's adviser _____ before a congressional committee last week.

2. (*talk*) He _____ to the committee for a total of thirty-six hours.

3. (*answer*) He _____ many questions posed by the committee.

4. (*listen*) I _____ carefully to his testimony as it was broadcast on television.

5. (*discuss*) Afterwards, the committee members _____ their reactions.

6. (*report*) The news media _____ the hearings in detail.

Answers start on page 177.

Irregular Past Tense

Although most verbs use the *ed* ending to show the past tense, there are many common *irregular* verbs. These verbs change form without using *ed*. Here are some common examples:

Speak—The adviser **spoke** last week.
Give—He **gave** many hours of testimony.
See—I **saw** him on television.
Be (with *he, she, it,* and singular nouns)—His picture **was** in all the newspapers.
Be (with *we, you, they,* and plural nouns)—The other advisers **were** not in uniform.

To write correctly, you should know the correct spellings of *all* verbs with irregular past tenses. Take some time now to learn all of the past forms in the appendix on pages 167–168. Look at the heading "Past Forms."

Be especially careful with past forms that are commonly confused:

WRONG: I **seen** him.   He **come** here.   He **done** it.   He **when** home.
RIGHT: I **saw** him.   He **came** here.   He **did** it.   He **went** home.

——————————————— PRACTICE 2 ———————————————

Answer the following questions. Use the correct irregular past forms in your answers. Check the appendix on pages 167–168 if you are unsure of a correct form. The first one has been done for you.

1. When did you get up today?

   I got up at 6:30 this morning.

2. What did you eat for dinner last night?

3. What did you drink?

4. What TV shows did you see yesterday or the day before?

5. Where were you during the last storm?

6. When were your last classes?

Answers will vary.

Negatives and Questions

Did you **see** that program? No, I **did** not **see** it.

In the past tense, use the helping verb _____ plus the _____ form of the main verb for questions and negatives.

┌───┐
│   **For all past tense questions and negatives, use *did* + base form.**   │
└───┘

The contraction for *did not* is *didn't*. Think of it like this:

did n**o**t
did**n**'t

Once again, the verb *be* is an exception. You do not need to add helping verbs to *was not* or *were not*. Both these words can be formed into contractions:

was n**o**t   were n**o**t
was**n**'t   were**n**'t

─────────────── PRACTICE 3 ───────────────

As a rookie police officer, you must question witnesses about a robbery at the Six-Twelve convenience store. You write down all your questions first. Ask witnesses everything they can remember about the robbery and the robber. Write ten questions in the past tense.

EXAMPLE: _Did the robber have a gun?_

Answers will vary.

─────────────── PROOFREAD ───────────────

Your twelve-year-old child is writing a letter to a friend in another city and asks you for help on the grammar.

YOUR JOB: Find and correct the eleven past-tense errors in the paragraph.

Did you watched "Rookie" on television last night? I seen it then for the first time, and I did'nt thought too much of it. I been so uninterested that I when out to make a sandwich. When I come back ten minutes later, the show continue to bore me. How you liked it? Was you bored too?

Answers start on page 177.

─────────────── WRITING ASSIGNMENT ───────────────

Write a paragraph of approximately eight sentences about an unusual experience that happened in your past. Be sure to use the past tense correctly. Here are some suggested ideas: a special celebration, a dangerous situation, an embarrassing experience, or an event that made you feel proud.

FUTURE TENSE

What Will Be Will Be

Stella will have a baby next June.

INSIGHT

What tense is used in this simple sentence—past, present, or future? _____

Clearly, this sentence is about the future. The words *next June* give you a clue that this sentence is about the future. The word *will* plus the base form make the **future tense**.

Contractions can also be used in the future tense.

I will   he will   she will   it will   you will   they will
I'll   he'll   she'll   it'll   you'll   they'll

You can also form contractions using the negative form. The complete form is *will not*; the contraction is *won't*.

> The future tense is formed with *will* + base form: *I will stay.*
> The negative is formed using *will not* or *won't*: *He will not stay.*
> *You won't stay either.*

―――――――――――――― PRACTICE ――――――――――――――

Answer each question twice, the first time positively and the second time negatively. Either complete forms or contractions are *OK*. The first one has been done for you.

1. What will your favorite sports team do if it has a winning streak?

   The Orioles will continue to do well.

   The Orioles will not get overconfident.

2. What will your favorite sports team do if it has a losing streak?

3. What will the current president do when he leaves office?

4. What will the next president do differently from the current one?

5. What will you do the next time you are sick?

6. What will you do to keep yourself healthy in the future?

7. What will you do the next time a stranger asks you for spare change?

8. What will you do the next time a friend or relative asks for a large loan?

Answers will vary.

CONTINUOUS

Coming and Going

The verb *be* can be a main verb, and it can also be a helping verb. Study these examples:

1. Rescue workers **are working** to make sure all the evacuees are comfortable.
2. Firefighters **were working** to put out a fire at a chemical plant at 10:30 last night.
3. Tomorrow, insurance people **will be working** to assess the damages to the area as soon as it is safe.

INSIGHT

In each sentence, you see a different form of the helping verb *be*. Which main verb do you see in each sentence? _____

Now write the last three letters you see on the end of the main verb *working*: __ __ __

The helping verb *be* plus a main verb with *ing* is the form of the ***continuous***. The continuous means that an action is a continuing one. Let's examine each of the sample sentences above.

1. The first sentence is in ***present continuous***. It shows an action that is happening right now.

2. The second sentence is in ***past continuous***. It shows an action was continuing and was not yet completed. At 10:30 the firefighters were still in the process of putting out the blaze.

3. The third sentence is in ***future continuous***. It shows an action that will be continuing into the future. The insurance people will not finish their work tomorrow. They will still be in the process of working.

In the sentences above, the continuing action is *working*.

> **The continuous shows that an action is a continuing one.**
> **Use the correct form of *be* (*am, is, are, was, were, will be*)**
> **and add *ing* to the end of the main verb.**

─────────────── **PRACTICE** ───────────────

Rewrite each sentence, using the time clues to tell you if the sentence should be in past, present, or future continuous. The first one has been done for you.

1. I am working on my project.
   a. at this time yesterday

   <u>At this time yesterday, I was working on my project.</u>
   b. at this time tomorrow

   <u>I will be working on my project at this time tomorrow.</u>

2. Tim is sleeping.
   a. at nine o'clock last night
   b. when you come back from Virginia next week

3. You were shouting.
   a. right now
   b. as soon as you see that invoice

4. Ms. Kim will be waiting for her son.
   a. even as we speak
   b. last Tuesday at midnight

5. The limousines are arriving.
   a. by the time the champagne is uncorked
   b. by the time the chandeliers were installed

6. The hairdresser is bleaching Samantha's hair.
   a. as I passed by the salon
   b. at this time tomorrow

Answers start on page 177.

PRESENT PERFECT TENSE

Nobody's Perfect

1. David **has been** in prison for two months.
2. He **has started** a vocational program in air conditioning and refrigeration.

INSIGHT

Look at sentence 1. When did David go to prison? _____ ago. Is he still in prison? _____

The verb of this sentence—*has been*—is in the ***present perfect tense***. The present perfect shows that a situation started in the past (David went to prison two months ago) and continues into the present (he is still in prison now).

Now look at sentence 2. Has David already started the program? _____ Do you know *exactly* when he started? _____

Again, the verb—*has started*—is in the present perfect tense. This time, the present perfect is showing that something has happened recently (David has started a program), but it's not clear exactly when (yesterday? last week? two hours ago?).

> **The present perfect tense shows that a situation started in the past and continues into the present. It can also show that an action happened recently at an unmentioned time.**

Subject	Helping Verb	Main Verb
he, she, it, singular nouns	has	started
I, you, we, they, plural nouns	have	started

PRACTICE 1

Answer each question using the present perfect correctly. Be sure to write a *complete* sentence for your answer. The first one has been done for you.

1. How long have you **been** a student?

   I have been a student for fourteen years.

2. How long have you **lived** in your community?

3. How long have you **known** your husband/wife/boyfriend/girlfriend/best friend?

4. How long have you **had** your stereo/television?

5. What kinds of hobbies have you **been** busy with lately?

6. What movies have you **seen** lately?

Answers will vary.

Past Participles

The form the main verb takes in the present perfect tense is called the ***past participle***. There are two kinds of past participles:

1. Past participles that are the same as past tense forms
  A. All *ed* past forms are also past participles:
     I worked—I have worked
  B. Many irregular past forms are also past participles:
     she thought—she has thought

2. Past participles that are different from past tense forms
   they went—they have gone
   they swam—they have swum

Most past participles end in *ed*. However, a number of very common verbs fit into the second category and have irregular past participles. Take some time to learn these irregular verbs from the list in the appendix on page 168. Look at the heading "Past Participle."

Be careful not to mix up past tense forms and past participles:

> WRONG: I **gone** there.   I **have went** there.
> RIGHT: I **went** there.   I **have gone** there.

───────────────── PRACTICE 2 ─────────────────

Write the correct present perfect form of the verb in parentheses. Use the correct helping verb (*have* or *has*) and the correct past participle.

  1. (*be*) Victor _____ both depressed and pleased lately.

  2. (*be*) He _____ in prison for two years.

  3. (*marry*) His girlfriend _____ someone else.

  4. (*stop*) Many of his friends _____ writing to him.

  5. (*make*) On the other hand, Victor _____ some important changes.

  6. (*begin*) For one thing, he _____ to learn a useful trade.

  7. (*work*) He _____ well on the appliances so far.

  8. (*go*) He _____ to five classes already.

  9. (*take*) He _____ a battery of aptitude tests.

 10. (*indicate*) The tests _____ he has a talent for understanding how appliances are put together.

 11. (*see*) Victor _____ that he can be doing something constructive with his life.

 12. (*decide*) He _____ to do the best he can to become an honest and dependable repairman.

Answers start on page 177.

Contractions

The verb *have* can be contracted:

I (have) worked   She (has) gone
I (')ve worked   She (')s gone

The negative form can also be contracted:

I have (not) worked   She has (not) gone
I haven(')t worked   She hasn(')t gone

Continuous

1. He has lived here for two months.
2. He has been living here for two months.

Both the sentences above are in the present perfect. Write the helping and main verbs for sentence 1 here: _____ _____

Now write the helping and main verbs for sentence 2 here: _____ _____ _____

You're right if you wrote *has lived* for sentence 1 and *has been living* for sentence 2. Sentence 2 uses present perfect in the continuous (*be* + the *ing* form). Both sentences have the same meaning, but sentence 2 emphasizes that the action is still going on in the present. This is how present perfect in the continuous differs from simple present perfect.

As with all verbs in the continuous, you need to use a form of the verb *be* with the *ing* form. That form should be the past participle *been*. Look at the chart below:

Subject	Helping Verb	Main Verb
he, she, it, singular nouns	has been	working
I, you, we, they, plural nouns	have been	working

PROOFREAD

You are the editor of a newspaper. One of your reporters has submitted a short article about a prison education program.

YOUR JOB: Correct the nine errors in present perfect tense. The first one has been done for you.

David and Victor are inmates at Halsted Prison. So far, David ~~have~~ has

served two months, and Victor has serve two years. Recently, both men be

studying in an education program at the prison called Project Workforce.

Project Workforce been in effect for only a year at Halsted, but already over

twenty volunteers from business and industry have been help as tutors. In

addition to attending state-sponsored vocational classes, inmates meet

individually with their tutors several times per week. David says, "I have

learned a lot in just a few weeks." Victor notes that they have demand a lot

of work, but he hasnt gave up yet.

Answers start on page 177.

PAST PERFECT TENSE

Time Had Not Stood Still

By the time Pam arrived at Shannon's,
the party **had ended**.

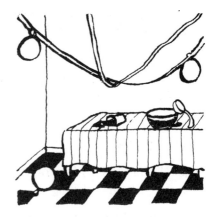

INSIGHT

Did Pam make it to the party on time? _____

Which of these actions happened *first?* (Circle one.)   **a.** Pam arrived   **b.** the party ended

You're right if you saw that Pam arrived *after* the party—the party had ended first. Think for a minute about these two actions.

Both actions happened in the past, but one happened *before* another. The event closest to the present (Pam arrived) uses the normal past tense, but the *earlier* action (the event that happened farthest back in the past) uses the **past perfect tense**.

The form of the past perfect tense is easy: the helping verb *had* plus the past participle.

> **Use the past perfect for a past event that happened before another past event.**
> **Use *had* + the past participle.**

——————————— PRACTICE 1 ———————————

Write the correct past perfect form of the verbs in parentheses.

1. (*end*) By the time Pam arrived, the party _____.

2. (*leave*) Pam showed up at 1:00 A.M. after all the guests _____.

3. (*drink*) Shannon offered Pam a glass of water because the guests _____ all the wine and soft drinks.

4. (*eat*) Shannon wanted to offer Pam some food, but the guests _____ everything except a few pretzels.

5. (*be*) Even though she was the only guest, Pam stayed until 2:30. By the time she finally went home, Shannon's husband _____ asleep on the sofa for half an hour.

6. (*wait*) There weren't many buses running at that hour. Finally, a bus pulled up at about 4:00 A.M. By that point, Pam _____ over an hour.

Answers start on page 178.

Contractions and Continuous

The word *had* can be contracted:

   They had waited   She had arrived

   They'd waited   She'd arrived

The negative form can also be contracted:

   They had not stayed

   They hadn't stayed

You can also use *had been* plus the *ing* form to show continuous action:

   I had been thinking about the fight with my boss when I broke the dish.

————————————— PRACTICE 2 —————————————

Pam is late for everything. Copy and complete each sentence about her, using the past perfect correctly. Remember that when you use the past perfect, you are talking about the *earlier* action. The first one has been done for you.

1. By the time she arrived at her friend's house, . . . _By the time she arrived at her friends house, the party had ended._

2. By the time she got to the meeting room, . . .

3. . . . when she entered the classroom.

4. Before she could get to the airport, . . .

5. When she arrived at the train station, . . .

6. . . . by the time she reached the theater.

Answers will vary.

More Work with Past Perfect

The past tense and the past perfect tense are frequently confused. Some people mistakenly think that they should always use the past perfect instead of the past tense because it sounds more "sophisticated" to do this. The result instead may be confusion on the part of the reader.

To avoid this problem, be sure that when you do use the past perfect, you have a good reason to do so. Remember that the past perfect is used for a past event that happened *before* another past event or time; it shows a *relationship* between the earlier and the later event.

To illustrate the problem and the solution, look at the following situations. Be sure you see why the first sentence is wrong and the other three are right.

SITUATION: Two past events at the same time

    WRONG: I **had eaten** five hamburgers last Friday. I also **drank** two shakes.
    RIGHT: I **ate** five hamburgers last Friday. I also **drank** two shakes.

SITUATION: Two past events at different times

    RIGHT: I **avoided** hamburgers last Saturday because I **had eaten** five hamburgers last Friday.
    RIGHT: I **had eaten** five hamburgers by the time I **started** in on the pizza.

Is it absolutely necessary to use the past perfect for the earlier of two past events? Not always. Frequently, especially in casual speech, only the past tense is used:

> The airplane **took** off before Pam arrived.

However, by using the past perfect, you can make your writing more emphatic and more formal:

> The airplane **had taken** off before Pam arrived.

––––––––––––––––––– PRACTICE 3 –––––––––––––––––––

Complete the sentences using the past tense and the past perfect correctly. Remember to use the past perfect for the earlier of the actions. You may need one tense or both tenses. The first one has been done for you.

1. By the time I _got_ (get) to the mall, I had cashed (cash) my paycheck already.

2. I _____ (have) $200 in my pocket, but I _____ (know) I shouldn't spend all of it right away.

3. First, I stopped at the shoe store. When I _____ (walk) out of the store, I _____ (buy) two pairs of shoes and some leather boots.

4. Next, I _____ (go) to the children's store and _____ (buy) a little outfit for my niece.

5. After that, I _____ (decide) it was time for lunch, so I _____ (eat) a large taco salad.

6. I _____ (spend) every penny by the time I _____ (leave) the mall.

Answers start on page 178.

––––––––––––––––––– WRITING ASSIGNMENT –––––––––––––––––––

When Pam arrived home after the party, she was shocked to find her children still awake and the babysitter sound asleep. The apartment was a terrible mess. Copy and complete this paragraph about all of the terrible things the children had done to the place. You can also mention the things they *hadn't* done. Use the past perfect to show that all of these things had happened *before* Pam arrived home. Use your imagination, and write at least ten sentences.

> When Pam arrived home, she received a terrible shock. The children had made a terrible mess.

TENSE CHOICE IN A PASSAGE

Don't Tense Up

When you start to write, you need to have a clear idea of what you are going to say. Are you going to talk about events of the past, present, future, or a combination of these times? This is a decision you must make *before* you begin writing.

The following passage shows what happens when the writer doesn't think about the tense first (and doesn't take the time to proofread after writing!):

> At the Martin Paper Company, I **worked** as a receptionist for two years. I **answer** the telephone, **transfer** calls, and **gave** out general information. I also **greeted** visitors to the company and **notify** the proper persons of their arrival. This position **is** very satisfying because I **was** able to help the company function smoothly.

INSIGHT

Is the writer talking about a job she has now or one she had in the past? Because the writer started in the past tense, you probably assumed that she was talking about a job she had in the past. You probably got confused when you got to the second sentence, which is in the present. What kind of impression would this make on a job application?

The writer should have kept the tense in mind as she was writing. Let us assume that the writer no longer has this job. She should say to herself: "This job was in the past. I am no longer working there." Then she would write the paragraph this way:

> At the Martin Paper Company, I **worked** as a receptionist for two years. I **answered** the telephone, **transferred** calls, and **gave** out general information. I also **greeted** visitors to the company and **notified** the proper persons of their arrival. This position **was** very satisfying because I **was** able to help the company function smoothly.

Could the writer use the *past perfect* tense somewhere while discussing this past job? Certainly—as long as she is discussing one past action before another. For example, she might add:

> Before I received this position, I **had worked** in the shipping department.

> **As you write (and as you proofread your work), use the appropriate tense.**

────────────── PRACTICE 1 ──────────────

Go back to the sample paragraph about the Martin Paper Company. Now imagine that the person is *still* working there. Rewrite it correctly, using the appropriate tense.

Answers start on page 178.

How to Switch Tenses

It is possible to write a paragraph about the past and include a sentence or two in the present tense or present perfect. You just have to make sure you have a good reason to do this. The following paragraph is a good example:

> **(1)** Today, there **are** laws that **protect** the consumer against fraud. **(2)** A hundred years ago, however, consumers **were** often the victims of false advertising. **(3)** Some companies, for example, **proclaimed** that their tonics **cured** baldness. **(4)** The tonics **did not work**, but people **bought** them anyway because they **believed** the deceptive labels. **(5)** Fortunately, much **has changed** since that time.

This paragraph is mainly about the (circle one)   **a.** past   **b.** present   **c.** future

This paragraph is mainly about the past. However, sentence 1 uses the _____ tense, and sentence 5 uses the _____ _____ tense.

Even though the paragraph is chiefly about the past and uses the past tense, two other tenses are used—the present and the present perfect. In sentence 1 the writer is specifically talking about today, so the present tense is appropriate. In sentence 5, the writer is talking about changes that began in the past and have continued to the present, so the present perfect is appropriate.

> **If you change tenses within a paragraph, be sure you have a good reason to do so.**

─────────────────── **PRACTICE 2** ───────────────────

Write the correct forms of the verbs in parentheses.

In the past, doctors _____ (be) not always able to treat illnesses

1

partly because they _____ (know) little about their causes. Since the

2

turn of the century, doctors _____ (learn) a great deal about

3

the causes of disease. For example, doctors now _____ (know) that

4

viruses cause many diseases. We now _____ (have) vaccines to prevent

5

smallpox and polio, two viral infections. Unfortunately, even though today's

doctors _____ (understand) the causes of certain diseases,

6

they _____ (be) not always able to find a cure for each one. So far,

7

scientists _____ (find) no cure for certain viral infections

8

ranging from the common cold to AIDS. Perhaps

they _____ (find) vaccines in the near future.

9

Answers start on page 178.

Show What You Know

You have learned how to use different tenses in sentences and in paragraphs. Now you'll have a chance to write an essay of two paragraphs in which you can concentrate on the correct use of tenses. Make each paragraph six to eight sentences long. Choose *one* of these topics:

1. Write about your work history. Describe your past jobs and your responsibilities in these positions. If you are currently employed, also describe your present job and your responsibilities.

2. Write about your fears. Describe your childhood fears, your present fears, and any fears that you might have had all your life.

3. Write about one of your children. Describe this child's personality and interests from birth to the present.

4. Write about your relationship with one of your siblings (sister or brother). Describe how you and this person got along as children and how you get along now.

When you are finished writing, proofread your paragraph for the following:

☑ Make sure you have used a good variety of sentences: simple, compound, and complex.
☑ Make sure all your sentences are complete and that there are no run-ons or fragments.
☑ Make sure that you have used the correct tense and that you changed tenses *only* when there was a good reason to do so.

CHAPTER 5
OTHER VERB ISSUES

Goals

- To avoid using *ain't* and double negatives
- To use the conditional form correctly
- To write quoted and reported speech correctly, including using quotation marks correctly

AVOIDING *AIN'T*

I'm Not Misbehaving

What is wrong with these sentences?

1. He ain't telling the truth.
2. We ain't listened to anything he has said.

INSIGHT

In each sentence above, which word is wrong? _____ The word *ain't* should never be used in any situation where standard English is used. Which words should be used instead of *ain't*? Go back and see if you already know how to correct the two sample sentences. You were right if you fixed them like this:

He **is not** telling the truth.
We **have not** listened to anything he has said.

> Never use the word *ain't*.
> Instead, use the verbs *am/is/are not* or the helping verbs *have/has not*.

How do you know which word must replace *ain't*? Look at the form of the *main verb* used in the sentence. Study these examples:

> WRONG: He **ain't** going there now.
> RIGHT: He **isn't** going there now.

Going ends in *ing*, so you need the helping verb *is*.

> WRONG: He **ain't** gone there yet.
> RIGHT: He **hasn't** gone there yet.

Gone is a past participle, so you need the helping verb *has*.

─────────────── **PRACTICE** ───────────────

Correct each sentence by replacing *ain't* with the right helping verb. Remember to use *have/has not* with the past participle. Use *am/is/are not* with the *ing* form. The first one has been done for you.

1. He ~~ain't~~ *isn't* telling the truth.

2. He ain't told anyone the truth about the situation.

3. I ain't heard whether or not anyone has discovered the actual facts.

4. He ain't going to retain his current position.

5. We ain't planning to encourage his behavior.

6. We ain't gone to the proper authorities yet.

7. You ain't being very helpful.

8. You ain't been listening to what I've been saying.

Answers start on page 178.

MORE WORK WITH NEGATIVES

Make No Bones About It

He did not tell her anything about his past.

INSIGHT

Did he tell her about his past? _____ The answer is *no*, so this is a negative sentence. Which word shows you the sentence is negative? _____ The word *not* shows the sentence is negative. Just one word makes the entire simple sentence negative—you don't need any other negative words. Look at the next sentence:

He told her nothing about his past.

This time, which word tells you the sentence is negative? _____ In this sentence, the word *nothing* makes the entire simple sentence negative.

Both of the sentences above are simple sentences. There is just one clause in a simple sentence because a simple sentence has just one S-V pair. In a compound or complex sentence, there are two or more clauses. There can be one negative word per clause. Look at the examples.

She **didn't** ask, so he **didn't** tell her.
Because they said **nothing** about their pasts, **neither** one knew.

The following words or word parts are negative: *no, not, -n't, never,* and *neither*.

Just one word makes an entire clause negative.
No, not, -n't, never, and *neither* are all negative words or word parts.

————————————————— PRACTICE 1 —————————————————
Circle the negative word in each sentence or clause.

1. He didn't tell her anything about his past.

2. She knew nothing of his former life.

3. She could not guess what he had done, and she didn't want to know.

4. He had no intention of divulging his secret to her.

5. He wanted nobody but her, and he didn't want to lose her.

6. If she did not approve of him, she wouldn't stay with him.

7. Of his past experiences, he told her nothing.

8. She never told him about her past, either.

9. Neither one knew the truth about the other.

Answers start on page 178.

Double Negatives

What is wrong with these sentences? (Hint: underline all of the negative words.)

   1. She didn't know nothing about him.
   2. She didn't know nothing, and he didn't tell her, neither.

Each clause contains a ***double negative***. In sentence 1, the simple sentence has two negative words: *didn't* and *nothing*. In sentence 2, the compound sentence has two negative words in each clause: *didn't* and *nothing*, *didn't* and *neither*.

How can these sentences be corrected? The easiest way is to eliminate one of the negatives:

   1. She **knew** nothing about him.
   2. She didn't know **anything**, and he didn't tell her, **either**.

How can you avoid a double negative? You can use these words or word parts instead of that second negative: *a, an, any, ever,* and *either*.

Use only one negative word per clause.

―――――――――――――――――― PRACTICE 2 ――――――――――――――――――

Use the following words to write your own sentences. Remember to avoid double negatives. The first one has been done for you.

1. any *I don't want to hear any criticism.*

2. don't/anything   **5.** no one

3. haven't/ever   **6.** can't/anyone

4. never   **7.** nothing

Answers will vary.

―――――――――――――――――― PROOFREAD ――――――――――――――――――

Your nosy neighbor Thelma likes to write all the neighborhood gossip in weekly letters to her elderly mother. She shows you her latest one and asks you for help on the grammar.

YOUR JOB: Correct the twelve *ain't* and double negative errors.

   Our neighbor Stella hadn't never expected this surprise. She hadn't heard none of the stories about her new beau, Sidney. We had tried to tell her, but she would not listen to none of us. She always said, "I ain't paid attention to your stories before, and I ain't going to start now." Sidney never told her nothing about his marriage to Ma Bailey, the famous counterfeiter. He didn't say nothing about his role in the bank robbery, neither. When Ma Bailey came back to find her man, Stella couldn't say not one word. She hadn't never been so shocked. Finally, she opened her mouth and said, "Good-bye Sidney. You ain't never going to see me again!"

Answers start on page 178.

CONDITIONAL

What If...?

1. In general, Jane doesn't seem to understand her son. If she **understood** him, she **would be** more sympathetic.
2. Jane didn't know that her son had tried to pay for the broken window last week. If she **had** known, she **would have** forgiven him.

INSIGHT

Is example 1 talking about a present problem or a past problem? _____ It describes a present situation: Jane doesn't understand her son *now*. The sentence that follows then describes an imaginary situation. You are asked to *imagine* how Jane would feel now if she really did understand her son.

Is example 2 talking about a present or past problem? _____ It describes a past problem: last week Jane didn't know of her son's attempt to pay. The next sentence describes an imaginary situation about the past. You are asked to *imagine* what Jane would have done if she had really known the facts.

The second sentences in examples 1 and 2 are in the **conditional**—complex sentences with a main clause and a dependent clause starting with *if*. These sentences express what the writer *imagines* about situations.

The box below shows how to construct sentences in the conditional.

	Dependent clause	Main clause
Conditional sentence—**present** situation	past tense	*would* + base form
	If I wanted your opinion,	I would ask for it.
Conditional sentence—**past** situation	past perfect	*would have* + past participle
	If I had known you better,	I would not have married you.

Note that the helping verb *would* can be contracted:

he would   he would not
he'd   he wouldn't

As in any complex sentence, the dependent clause can come first or last:

If she understood him, she would be more sympathetic.
She would be more sympathetic **if she understood him.**

———————————— PRACTICE 1 ————————————

Copy and complete each conditional sentence about a present or past situation. Use the correct verb forms. The first one has been done for you.

1. If I needed your help, . . .

   If I needed your help, I would ask for it. _____

2. If I had known every answer on the test, . . .

3. If I needed to borrow $500, . . .

4. If I wanted to go to a different school, . . .

5. If I had been sick last week, . . .

6. If I had missed that party, . . .

7. If I had overslept yesterday, . . .

———————————— PRACTICE 2 ————————————

Copy and complete each conditional sentence about the present or past. The first one has been done for you.

1. I would tell you if . . .

   I would tell you if you needed to know. _____

2. I would have helped you if . . .   5. I would have cried if . . .

3. I would move to a new place if . . .   6. I would have been thrilled if . . .

4. I would take a vacation now if . . .   7. I would have been very surprised if . . .

Answers will vary.

The Verb *Be*

> If I **were** rich, I would buy a house.

This conditional sentence is about an imagined situation in the present: the truth is that I am not rich, but I can imagine what I would do if I were.

Does the verb *were* seem strange? Normally the past tense form for *I* is *was*. However, in the present conditional, *were* is used for all subjects:

> If I **were** rich, I would buy a house.
> If she **were** rich, she would travel around the world.
> If they **were** rich, they would help all of their relatives.

Use *were* for all subjects in the present conditional.

This rule is also true when the verb *be* is used as a helping verb, as in this example:

> If I **were moving** to Cincinnati, I would become a Bengals fan.

———————————— PRACTICE 3 ————————————

Copy and complete each sentence. The first one has been done for you.

1. If I were rich, . . .

If I were rich, I would move to the Bahamas.

2. If I were on vacation now, . . .

3. If I weren't here right now, . . .

4. If I were . . .

5. If I weren't . . .

Answers will vary.

A Common Problem

Something is wrong with this sentence:

If I had won the lottery last week, I would of bought a car.

Which word is wrong? _____ Which helping verb should have been used instead? _____ When spoken quickly, the word *have* can sound like *of*, so it is easy to make a mistake in this situation. Remember to write the complete form *have* or the contraction *'ve*:

. . . I would **have** bought a car.
. . . I **would've** bought a car.

The same holds true for other helping verbs such as *could, should,* and *might* and their negative forms.

> **Always write *would have, could have*, and so on.**
> **Never write *would of, could of*, and so on.**

———————————— PROOFREAD ————————————

Your drama class is writing a skit about Lord and Lady Highbrow. You go over the dialogue carefully.

YOUR JOB: Correct the six errors in the conditional sentences.

LADY H: You are making a fool of yourself by flirting with the governess. If she was the slightest bit interested in you, I would be flabbergasted. Of course, you know that I leave you here and now if I found the two of you together!

LORD H: My darling, rest assured that I love only you. If I love the governess, I would ask you for a divorce this very day! You know I am an honest man!

LADY H: Oh, why did I marry you? If I had married the king, I would of been happy!

LORD H: Ah, but you are *not* a queen. Anyway, if the king was your husband, you'd still find something to complain about.

LADY H: If I was the queen, I would have no complaints. And now, dear man, you are giving me a royal pain. Be off!

Answers start on page 178.

QUOTED SPEECH

You Can Quote Me on That

The senator said, "My constituents can trust me. I will not vote against their wishes."

INSIGHT

The senator made two statements, and the writer has quoted them word for word. A **quote** is the speaker's exact words. Circle the punctuation marks before and after the senator's words.

You should have circled a comma, a period, and a pair of **quotation marks** (" . . . "). Note that the senator said two complete sentences. These are punctuated like all statements, with periods at the end. The last period comes *before* the quotation mark. Of course, each sentence begins with a capital letter.

> **When you write down a quote, follow this form:**
> (speaker) said, "_____."

—————————————— PRACTICE 1 ——————————————

Add capital letters, commas, and quotation marks to the sentences below. The first one has been done for you.

1. The senator said, "My constituents can have the fullest confidence that I will not vote against them."

2. She said the rebels are not supported by their own people, so they do not deserve our support.

3. The other senator added these so-called freedom fighters are simply glorified terrorists.

4. The vice president protested these men are fighting for democracy and are not terrorists.

5. The reporter asked will this country continue to support the rebels?

Answers start on page 179.

Punctuating When the Quote Is First

Circle the punctuation in the sample sentences below:

> "What is your opinion?" asked the reporter.
> "The war is wrong," said the senator.

INSIGHT

Once again, quotation marks are used around the quotes. However, in the second sentence, a comma (instead of a period) appears at the end of the quote. This happens because the speaker appears at the *end* of the sentence.

> **When the speaker appears at the end of the sentence, use a comma instead of a period at the end of the quote. "_____," said (speaker).**
> **If the quote is a question, a question mark goes at the end of the quote.**

───────────── PRACTICE 2 ─────────────

Add correct punctuation and capital letters. The first one has been done for you.

1. The war is wrong, said the senator.

2. What about the struggle for democracy asked the reporter.

3. The senator replied democracy already exists in that land. The current president was elected by the people.

4. That is simply not true retorted the protest leader.

5. What evidence do you have asked the reporter.

Answers start on page 179.

Continuing the Quote

Look at the following examples:

1. "The evidence," said the protester, "is overwhelming."
2. "I heartily disagree," said the vice president. "The evidence is inconclusive."

INSIGHT

Notice that both examples 1 and 2 have quotes that are interrupted by *said* phrases (such as *said the protester*). Go back now and circle the commas and periods in the sentences above. Then underline any capital letters.

You may have noticed that the second part of the quote begins with a capital letter in example 2 but not in example 1. Let's look only at the words of the protester and the senator to discover why:

1. The evidence is overwhelming.
2. I heartily disagree. The evidence is inconclusive.

How many sentences do you see in example 1? _____ In example 2? _____ In a quote like example 1, there is just one sentence. You know that a sentence always has a capital letter at the beginning and a period at the end. The sentence is simply interrupted by the phrase *said the protester*. To set off this phrase from the rest of the sentence, the phrase is surrounded with commas. (The first one is *inside* the quotation marks, as you learned before).

Now let's examine example 2. This quote has *two* sentences. The first sentence ends before the phrase *said the vice president*, so a period goes after that phrase.

"I heartily disagree," said the vice president.

The second sentence, like all complete sentences, must start with a capital letter:

"The evidence is inconclusive."

One-Sentence Quotes
"_____," said (speaker), "_____."
Use one capital letter at the very beginning of the entire sentence.

Two-Sentence Quotes
"_____," said (speaker). "_____."
Use a capital letter at the beginning of *each* sentence.

─────────────────── PRACTICE 3 ───────────────────

Below is a list of quotes. Some have one sentence, and others have two. Add correct punctuation and capital letters accordingly. Don't forget the punctuation at the very end! The first one has been done for you.

1. "The war, proclaimed the senator, is wrong."

2. i don't understand she said please explain your view

3. the people will win said the protester we cannot keep them down

4. i support the rebels said the vice president and so should all of us

5. i cannot agree with you the senator replied this is an ill-advised policy

6. in the last few months he said hundreds have fled

7. the living conditions were bad before he added however, they are even worse now

8. starvation and violence said the volunteer are ravaging the population

9. we can do nothing she continued we can only wait and watch

10. although the situation is bad she said there is still hope

Answers start on page 179.

REPORTED SPEECH

Accurate Reporting

Ms. Park said that she was ready to go.

INSIGHT

In this sentence, is the writer giving us a quote—telling Ms. Park's *exact* words? _____ Do you see quotation marks? _____ This sentence does *not* quote Ms. Park directly. Ms. Park's exact words were probably "*I am* ready to go." The sample sentence above merely reports the *ideas* that she expressed. This is called *reported speech.*

Notice that in the reported speech above the pronoun *I* changes to _____ because the writer is now talking *about* Ms. Park, instead of quoting her exact words. Notice that the present tense (*am*) in the quote changes to the _____ tense (*was*) in reported speech. In effect, in going from quoted speech to reported speech, you take a step farther back in the past.

> **To change quoted speech to reported speech,**
> **move the verb tenses one step into the past.**

Quoted Speech	Reported Speech	Examples*
present	past	He said, "I understand." He said that he understood.
past	past perfect	He said, "I ate." He said he had eaten.
present perfect	past perfect	He said, "I have eaten." He said he had eaten.
can	could	He said, "I can do it." He said that he could do it.
will	would	He said, "I will do it." He said that he would do it.

*Note: The word *that* is optional.

─────────────── **PRACTICE 1** ───────────────

Copy and complete each sentence in reported speech. Make the correct verb and pronoun changes. Think about the meaning! Do *not* use quotation marks. The first one has been done for you.

1. Ms. Park said, "I am ready to go."
Ms. Park announced that . . . .

Ms. Park announced that she was ready to go.

2. She said, "I have all of my notes."
She said that . . . .

3. She said, "I have practiced my presentation several times."
She told Mr. Sulik that . . . .

4. Mr. Sulik said, "The audience will ask certain questions."
Mr. Sulik noted that . . . .

5. He said, "I will handle the difficult questions."
He promised that . . . .

6. Ms. Park said, "I can answer them myself."
Ms. Park reassured him that . . . .

7. Ms. Park said, "I wrote a list of possible questions."
Ms. Park mentioned that . . . .

8. Mr. Sulik said, "You are a valuable employee."
Mr. Sulik told her that . . . .

Answers start on page 179.

Reported Questions

What happens when questions are reported? Take a look at the examples below:

> The manager said, "Why do the boxes look so sloppy?"
> The manager asked **why the boxes looked so sloppy**.

As with reported statements, the present tense (*do look*) changes to the past tense (*looked*). There is an additional change as well: the question has been changed into a statement. Notice that the helping verb and the question mark are no longer needed. Question words like *why*, *when*, *where*, *who*, and *how* appear at the beginning of the reported speech. Take a look at another example:

> The manager said, "Are the boxes heavy?"
> The manager asked **if the boxes were heavy**.

The word *if* appears when there is no question word.

What is wrong with this sentence?

> Melba asked Anthony did he want to have lunch with her.

Even though the writer has not put a question mark at the end of this sentence, the reported speech is still phrased the way a question would be. Remember to change questions into statements:

Melba asked Anthony **if he wanted to have lunch with her**.

In reported questions, change the question into a statement.
The word *if* or a question word like *why, where, how*, etc.,
begins the reported question.

─────────────── PRACTICE 2 ───────────────

Darcy, also known as the company bootlicker, overhears two coworkers, Alba and Zack, flirting on the job.

ZACK: Where do you want the boxes?
ALBA: You can carry them up to the sixth floor.
ZACK: Have you ever lifted an elephant?
ALBA: You are a real comedian.
ZACK: Do you want to marry me?
ALBA: I will marry you on one condition.
ZACK: What is it?
ALBA: I will tell you after you get back from the sixth floor.

Darcy decides to report the entire conversation to the boss, Mr. Sulik. Copy and complete Darcy's report to Mr. Sulik, using reported speech correctly. Do *not* use quotation marks or question marks. The first sentence has been written for you.

I just overheard Alba and Zack carrying on and wasting time. First, Zack asked Alba where she wanted the boxes.

Answers start on page 179.

─────────────── WRITING ASSIGNMENT ───────────────

Choose *one* topic:

1. Think of a conversation that drew you and your boyfriend/girlfriend/husband/wife closer together.

2. Think of a conversation you had with a friend or relative you hadn't seen in a long time.

Write a paragraph of about ten sentences reporting this conversation. Include some reported questions. Do not use quotation marks or question marks.

CUMULATIVE REVIEW

Show What You Know

Choose one of these topics and write two paragraphs of about eight sentences each. As you write, try to use the following in *some* of your sentences:

- conditionals
- quoted and reported speech

1. Describe what you would do if you won a million dollars.

2. Think of two people you know (or imagine two people)—husband and wife *or* parent and teenager—who have just had an argument. Describe the problem from the point of view of each of the two people. In other words, tell how each person saw the situation.

When you have finished writing, proofread your paper.

☑ Check that all your sentences are complete and there are no run-ons and fragments.
☑ Check that you have used a variety of sentence types: simple, compound, and complex.
☑ Check to be sure that you have not used *ain't* or any double negatives.

CHAPTER 6
AGREEMENT

BASIC AGREEMENT

Being Agreeable

You already know something about subject-verb agreement. Look at these examples:

1. Mr. McDonald _____ a bookkeeper. (*am? is? are?*)
2. He _____ downtown. (*work? works?*)

INSIGHT

In sentence 1, of course, the correct answer is *is*. In sentence 2, the answer is *works*. These verbs *agree* with their subjects.

Subject-verb agreement is important in the present tense, in the present perfect tense, and with the verb *be* in the present and past tenses. In other tenses, the verb form does not change for different subjects.

> PRESENT: I work. He work**s**.
> PRESENT PERFECT: I **have** gone. She **has** gone.
> THE VERB *be*: I **am** home. We **are** home.
> I **was** lonely. They **were** lonely.

Of course, for these tenses, the helping verbs in negative sentences and questions must also agree with their subjects. For example, in the present tense, it's *he doesn't* but *they don't*. It's *does he. . .?* but *do they. . .?*

You may wish to review the chapter on verb tenses on pages 85–103 before you go on in this chapter.

> **Make sure that your verbs agree with your subjects when you use the present tense, the present perfect tense, and the verb *be*.**

118

INTERRUPTING PHRASE OR CLAUSE

Time Out for Interference

Subject-verb agreement can get tricky at times. Try this problem:

Insurance for people without jobs _____ often expensive. (*is*? *are*?)

INSIGHT

To decide which verb is right for the sentence, you'll first need to find the subject.

What is the subject of this sentence? In other words, which will be expensive—*insurance, people,* or *jobs*? _____

You're right if you said that *insurance* is the subject. The writer is saying that insurance can be expensive. Therefore, *is* is the correct verb for the sentence because the verb *is* agrees with the singular subject *insurance.*

The words *for people without jobs* make up a phrase that tells us more about insurance. This phrase adds meaning to the subject, but it is not a part of the subject. When you are trying to make verbs agree with subjects, you should ignore any phrases or clauses that come between the subject and the verb. Think of the sample sentence like this:

Insurance (for people without jobs) is often expensive.

> **When checking subject-verb agreement, ignore any phrases or clauses that come between the subject and the verb.**

——————————————— PRACTICE 1 ———————————————

Each sentence below is correct. Put parentheses around any phrase or clause that comes between the subject and verb. Then underline each subject and verb and connect them with a line. The first one has been done for you.

1. One disadvantage (of private policies) is the cost.

2. Group insurance from employers is less expensive.

3. Most people in a large company have group insurance.

4. Frequently, people who do part-time work lack insurance benefits.

5. A person without insurance benefits needs to pay for a private policy.

6. Individuals who cannot afford private insurance suffer when they have to pay medical bills.

———————————— PRACTICE 2 ————————————

Some of the sentences below are correct, and others have errors. If the sentence has an error, write the correct verb above the sentence. If the sentence is correct, mark *OK* in the blank. Hint: you may want to mark the sentences as you did in Practice 1 to help you decide. The first one has been done for you.

__OK__ 1. Some people who cannot afford their own insurance pay high medical bills.

_____ 2. Many people without insurance avoids medical care.

_____ 3. A person who has no insurance benefits suffer from high bills or bad medical care.

_____ 4. A company that offers insurance benefits provide a real service to its employees.

_____ 5. One advantage of working for large corporations is the access to insurance.

_____ 6. One disadvantage of part-time jobs are the lack of insurance benefits.

_____ 7. Sometimes people who dislike their full-time jobs hold on to them for the sake of the insurance benefits.

_____ 8. Medical bills even for a minor injury is often surprisingly high.

_____ 9. An insurance company that processes claims quickly is a big help to the consumer.

_____ 10. Unfortunately, paperwork that must go through many channels slow the process down.

Answers start on page 179.

TRICKY PRONOUNS

All Is Not One

Everything in the bedrooms _____ a mess. (*are*? *is*?)
Someone _____ to clean it up. (*have*? *has*?)

INSIGHT

When it comes to subject-verb agreement, pronouns like *everything* and *someone* can be tricky. The key is to look at the second part of each pronoun. Circle the word parts *thing* and *one* in the sentences above. (Remember that *everything* is the subject in sentence 1, not *bedrooms*.) Now ask yourself: Is *thing* singular or plural? _____ How about *one*? _____

You are right if you wrote *singular*. Any pronoun ending in the word parts *thing* or *one* will be singular. The same holds true for pronouns ending in *body*, such as *everybody* or *somebody*. With this in mind, let's look at the correct sentences:

Everything in the bedrooms **is** a mess.
Someone **has** to clean it up.

Can you think of other pronouns ending in *thing, one*, or *body*? Write them on the line. (Hint: *no one* is the only pronoun with two separate words.)

_____

_____

A pronoun ending in *one, body*, or *thing* is always singular.

Certain other words also are always singular. Be sure your verbs agree with these singular subjects:

Singular Word	Example
one	**One** of the girls **is** lazy.
each	**Each** of the boys **is** helpful.
either	**Either** of the twins **is** ready to help.
neither	**Neither** of the twins **is** lazy.

Note that in each of the sentences above, the words *one, each, either*, and *neither* are actually the subjects of the sentences. *Of the girls* and the other phrases are just interrupting phrases like the kind you studied on pages 119–120.

You have learned that certain words are always singular. Now study the words that are always plural:

Plural Word	Example
both	**Both** of my sisters **have** run in marathons.
many	**Many** of my friends **like** to jog.
several	**Several** of the runners **have** their knees or ankles wrapped.
few	**Few** of the contestants **think** of cheating.

———————————— PRACTICE 1 ————————————

Circle the correct verb or helping verb for each sentence.

1. Each of my brothers (*has/have*) different interests.

2. One of my brothers (*doesn't/don't*) agree with anyone about anything.

3. Both of my sisters (*appreciates/appreciate*) the same music.

4. Neither of them (*likes/like*) country music.

5. Families do not always share the same tastes. Many (*argues/argue*) about what music to play or what television show to watch.

6. (*Does/Do*) everyone in your family have the same taste?

7. Each family (*is/are*) different and (*resolves/resolve*) disagreements in a different way.

8. Somebody always (*refuses/refuse*) to go along with the others.

9. Nothing (*works/work*) to convince this type of person to be more accommodating.

Answers start on page 180.

———————————— PRACTICE 2 ————————————

Imagine that the apartment is a mess and everyone in the family has gathered to discuss the problem. Copy and complete the sentences about the situation, using the present tense. Be sure to make your verbs agree with the subjects. The first one has been done for you.

1. Everything in the apartment . . .

 Everything in the apartment is in disarray.

2. Everybody . . .

3. No one . . .

4. Nothing in the kitchen cabinets . . .

5. A few of the refrigerator shelves . . .

6. Every member of the family . . .

7. Both of the beds in the children's room . . .

8. One of the closets . . .

9. Neither of the bedrooms . . .

10. Each of the wastebaskets . . .

11. Many of the windows in the apartment . . .

Answers will vary.

Subjects That Can Be Singular or Plural

1. All of the dishes _____ dirty. (*is? are?*)
2. All of the food _____ spoiled. (*is? are?*)

If you wrote *All of the dishes are* . . . but *All of the food is* . . ., you were right. The word *all* can take a plural or singular verb form, depending on the noun in the describing phrase. In sentence 1, *all* refers to the plural *dishes*. In sentence 2, *all* refers to the noncount noun *food*. Noncount nouns use the same verb forms as singular nouns do, so here is how the sentences should look:

1. All of the dishes **are** dirty.
2. All of the food **is** spoiled.

The words *most, more, some, half, none,* and *any* act in the same way.

> **The words *all, most, more, some, half, none,* and *any***
> **can take singular or plural verb forms depending on the nouns they represent.**

—————————————————— **PRACTICE 3** ——————————————————

The refrigerator broke while you were out of town. Complete each sentence about the situation with *was* or *were*. Be sure your verbs agree with the subjects.

1. There was a whole carton of milk. When we got back, all of it _____ spoiled.

2. Most of the peaches in the plastic bag _____ rotten.

3. We had a lot of cheese. Now half _____ moldy.

4. None of the meat _____ still good.

5. Not all the food went bad. Fortunately, some _____ still edible.

6. A few of the apples were rotten, but some of them _____ still fresh and crisp.

—————————————————— **PROOFREAD** ——————————————————

Just when the refrigerator appears to be up and running, the washing machine and dryer completely fall apart. You decide to get organized and write down exactly how the family's laundry can get done without the benefit of your own washer and dryer.

YOUR JOB: Find and correct the ten errors in tricky subject pronouns. The first one has been done for you.

Our washer and dryer are broken beyond repair. Neither ~~are~~ *is* fixable

within our budget. Therefore, all of us is going to have to pitch in to get the

laundry done by other methods. Each of us need to volunteer one night a week to go to the laundromat. Nobody like to drag big bags of clothes to a laundromat, I know, so if some of the wash get done every night, everyone will have to do just one or two loads. A few of the things doesn't need to be machine washed. For instance, most of the underwear only have to be soaked in hot, soapy water, and each of Jeroma's many sweaters is better off anyway if hand washed. If someone have a problem with helping with the laundry, all of his or her things stays in the laundry hamper. I need all of you to cooperate. If everyone help, we can keep our household running smoothly.

Answers start on page 180.

TRICKY NOUNS

News for the Public

In this section, you will look at subject-verb agreement with tricky nouns. Some nouns end in *s* but are really singular, some nouns are always plural, and some are singular sometimes and plural at other times.

Tricky Singular Nouns

The news **is** good.

INSIGHT

The noun *news* ends in the letter *s*, but it is singular. Study this list:

> **Singular nouns that end in *s***
> athletics
> economics, mathematics, physics
>   (and other areas of study)
> news
> politics
> the United States

Here is another case in which the subject is always singular:

Five hours **is** not enough time to sleep.
Two million dollars **is** a lot of money.
Six miles **is** a long way to walk.

Even though *hours*, *dollars*, and *miles* are plural nouns by themselves, they are treated as singular when they are used as amounts or measures.

Amounts and measures are treated as singular nouns.

Tricky Plural Nouns

Some nouns may look singular but are actually plural. Look at this example:

The homeless **need** our help.

INSIGHT

The subject here, *homeless*, is a shorter way of saying *homeless people*. *People*, of course, is a plural noun. Some other examples are *the rich, the poor, the elderly*, and *the needy*.

Some nouns are always plural and have no singular form. Look at these examples:

The bloody pants **were** an important clue.
The scissors **were** the murder weapon.

Nouns that are always plural
clothes
[eye]glasses
jeans, pants, shorts, slacks, trousers
scissors
police

Be careful! If you add the phrase *a pair of* to some of these words, *pair* becomes the subject. (The word *pair* is singular).

The **scissors were** the murder weapon.
A **pair** of scissors **was** the murder weapon.

─────────────── **PRACTICE 1** ───────────────

Write the correct present tense form of the verb in parentheses. Make sure your verbs agree with your singular or plural subjects.

1. (*have*) The United States _____ a number of problems in its cities.

2. (*need*) In most major cities, the homeless _____ more shelters.

3. (*be*) In addition, clothes _____ needed by the cities' poor.

4. (*become*) The police _____ overloaded and cannot respond to calls in time.

5. (*be*) Politics _____ often a corrupt business.

6. (*be*) Needless to say, a few months _____ not enough time to solve all the problems.

7. (*need*) The poor _____ to become more involved in coming up with solutions to these problems.

8. (*do*) Without the proper community involvement, even $100 billion _____ not guarantee a solution.

Answers start on page 180.

Collective Nouns

The audience _____ enthusiastic. (*was? were?*)

INSIGHT

The sentence above is a tricky one. Is the subject singular or plural? On the one hand, the word *audience* seems plural: it consists of many people. On the other hand, it seems singular: it is one group. *Audience* is a **collective noun**, a noun that refers to several people or things acting as a group.

Generally, collective nouns are singular. Think of them as one unit or a group acting as one. Therefore, you write *The audience was enthusiastic* because the audience behaved as one.

Sometimes, however, the members of a group do not behave as one. In this case, collective nouns are treated as plural, as in this example:

The audience **were** fighting among themselves.

Here the writer is discussing what different, individual members of the group were doing.

To avoid writing a confusing sentence, you may want to add a clarifying phrase:

The **people** in the audience **were** fighting among themselves.

Here the plural noun *people* has become the subject of the sentence.

> **Collective nouns are singular when they refer to a group acting as one.**

Here is a list of common collective nouns:

audience	collection	faculty	orchestra
band	committee	family	public
class	community	group	staff
club	crowd	jury	team

————————————— PRACTICE 2 —————————————

Copy and complete these sentences using the present tense. Be sure that your verbs agree with your subjects. The first one has been done for you.

1. The public . . .

   The public needs to be informed of dangerous weather.

2. My family . . .

3. The members of my family . . .

4. The team . . .

5. The players on the team . . .

6. The club . . .

7. The members of the club . . .

Answers will vary.

COMPOUND SUBJECTS

And/Or

1. Lee and Shanika are going to need the car tomorrow.
2. Lee or Shanika is going to pick it up from the shop.
3. Shanika or her parents are going to pay the bill.

INSIGHT

All three sentences above have compound subjects. Why, then, are the verbs different? Look back to sentence 1, and circle the word that connects the two parts of the subject. Do the same for sentences 2 and 3.

You should have circled *and* for 1 and *or* for 2 and 3. Sentence 1 clearly has a plural subject—it tells about *both* Lee and Shanika. All compound subjects with *and* are (circle one) **a.** singular **b.** plural.

The situation is trickier when it comes to compound subjects with *or*. In sentence 2, only *one* of the two people will get the car, so the subject is singular.

In sentence 3, however, either *one* person (Shanika) or *two* people (her parents) will pay the bill. In this case, the verb should agree with the part of the subject that comes closest to the verb. Here is how the sentence would read if the two parts of the subject were reversed:

Her parents or Shanika **is** going to pay the bill.

> A compound subject with *and* is always plural. In a compound subject with *or*, the verb should agree with the part of the subject that appears last.

————————————— PRACTICE —————————————

Read the sentences about a pair of roommates and their car problems. Write the correct present tense form of the verb to agree with the compound subject.

1. (*depend*) Shanika and Lee _____ on their car for transportation to work.

2. (*have*) When the car malfunctioned, Shanika took it to the shop, and now she or Lee _____ to call the mechanic to find out the extent of the repairs necessary.

3. (*be*) The engine and the transmission _____ not working properly.

4. (*need*) Also, the brake pads or the brakes _____ to be checked.

5. (*require*) On the driver's side, the hinges or maybe even the entire door _____ replacement.

6. (*be*) Only money orders or cash _____ accepted by the shop.

7. (*be*) Lee's savings and income _____ too low to contribute to the cost of car maintenance.

Answers start on page 180.

INVERTED SENTENCES

Here Comes Trouble

There _____ several problems with the product. (*is*? *are*?)
Here _____ an example of the problems. (*is*? *are*?)

INSIGHT

To know which verb form is correct for each of these sentences, of course you first need to find the subject. Where is it?

In sentences beginning with *here* or *there*, the subject comes right *after* the verb. Therefore, the word *problems* is the subject of the first sentence. What is the subject of the second sentence? _____ You are right if you wrote *example*. Now that you know the two subjects, you can fill in the correct verbs:

There **are** several problems with the product.
Here **is** an example of the problems.

> **In sentences starting with *here* or *there*, the subject comes after the verb.**

You have seen that in sentences with *here* and *there*, the subject comes after the verb. There are other types of sentences in which the verb comes before the subject. Circle the subject of each of these sentences:

1. Attached **is** a money order for the entire payment.
2. In the envelope **were** three checks.

If you circled *money order* and *checks*, you were correct. How do you know that these are the subjects? One way is to ask yourself these questions:

What is attached? *a money order*
What things were in the envelope? *three checks*

Another way to find the subjects is to reverse the order of the words:

Attached is a money order = A money order is attached
In the envelope were three checks = Three checks were in the envelope

Remember that words and phrases like *attached* and *in the envelope* are *not* subjects. They just give more information about the subjects.

Sentences that consist of this structure—

WORD OR PHRASE + VERB + SUBJECT

—are called ***inverted sentences*** because the word order is inverted: the subject comes after the verb.

———————————— PROOFREAD ————————————

It is the year A.D. 2050. Your family has just received a new Robo-Butler in the mail, but it arrived damaged. One family member has written a letter to the company to complain about the robot.

YOUR JOB: Correct the eight subject-verb agreement errors with inverted sentences. The first one has been done for you.

Dear Sir or Madam:

         are
The Robo-Butler that we purchased last week is defective. First, there ~~is~~ no instructions telling us how to operate the robot. In addition, there are only one mechanical arm instead of the three arms pictured in the ad. Finally, on the mechanical arm, there are only two fingers instead of five, and on one of the fingers are a broken joint.

For four days, we have tried unsuccessfully to telephone your toll-free number. The first time there was a busy signal, next there were a recorded message, and then for the last three days there have been no answer whatsoever. For this reason, we are writing a letter in the hope of a quick response. Please remember that there is many people dependent upon your robot service for three meals a day and a clean house!

Here are all the information you will need. Our Robo-Butler (Serial No. 53212-6) was purchased at Robot Shack in San Diego, California, on May 21 for $799.99. Enclosed is the receipts from the store and the credit company.

Thank you for your prompt attention.

Answers start on page 180.

A Common Problem

Which is the correct verb form here?

There _____ a broken joint and a missing handle. (*is*? *are*?)

Some people argue that standard English requires the verb *are* to agree with the compound subject *joint and . . . handle*. Others argue that the verb *is* sounds more natural since the first part of the compound subject is singular (*a broken joint*).

To many people, however, both options sound awkward. What can you do? Avoid the problem completely by rewriting the sentence! Here is an example:

The robot has a broken joint and a missing handle.

CUMULATIVE REVIEW

Show What You Know

You have studied some of the trickiest aspects of subject-verb agreement. Pull all your knowledge together as you do this next exercise.

———————————————————— **PROOFREAD** ————————————————————

As the editor of Sweet 'n' Savage Romance Books, you are ready to publish a new novel. As you reread the manuscript, you notice some problems with the last few pages.

YOUR JOB: Correct the twenty-one errors in subject-verb agreement. The first one has been done for you.

Cassandra and her trusted companion Eloise ~~was~~ *were* in mortal fear. The robber band were drawing closer by the minute. Soon, either Cassandra or Eloise were going to have to jump from the hiding place in the cliff to the swirling depths below.

Finally, Cassandra spoke. "You and I am in this together. No one are going to rescue us, so we must make a plan. Now, in my satchel is two pieces of rope. Tie them together and then lower me down to the sea."

"Yes, my lady," murmured Eloise, fumbling with the rope.

"Speak up, woman!" cried Cassandra. "Your murmurs and whispers is starting to get on my nerves. If you do not help me, everything are lost!"

"All of my hopes and wishes goes with you," Eloise said, a new determination in her voice. With that, she tied the rope around Cassandra's waist, and Cassandra slipped over the edge.

She hit the water and began to swim with all her strength. Suddenly, she looked up from the frothy waves. A boat with two men were making its way toward her. "My companion and I has come to save you!" one of the men were shouting.

"Dirk! Blithers! Thank goodness it is you!" she exclaimed as the two men pulled her into the boat.

Then she went on, "My news are not good. The robbers are after us. I jumped to get help, but Eloise remain above, cold and hungry."

Cassandra looked around. In the boat was warm clothes and other provisions. "Here is some sandwiches, my lady," said Blithers. "Eat hearty."

As she ate, she looked toward shore. "There are another person in the waves!" she cried. " 'Tis Eloise."

Moments later, both pairs of lovers was reunited. Each of the ladies were with her man. Their clothes was in rags and they had no money, but they was happy. "The poor is blessed when they are with the ones they love," said Dirk. He set sail, and the boat drifted to safety.

Answers start on page 180.

PRONOUN AGREEMENT

Who Is He?

You have seen how important subject-verb agreement is. Now you will work on a new kind of agreement: *pronoun agreement*. The following sentences appeared at the beginning of a student's report on a hobby:

> This is an excellent hobby for people with busy and stressful lives. Moreover, while it can provide hours of pleasure and relaxation, they do not require a lot of attention.

INSIGHT

Do you feel a bit confused? Can you tell what the writer is talking about? *Something* will provide relief from stress, and you certainly could use a little of that in your life! However, you are frustrated until you come to the next line:

> Daily watering and a place in the sun are their only needs.

Now you have a clue. The writer is talking about plants and indoor gardening. As the writer wrote, she used pronouns in a confusing way. Go back and circle each pronoun, including the word *this*, in her paragraph.

This? *It*? *They*? The writer knows what *she* means by these words, but the reader doesn't. To make her writing more understandable, the writer should have included a clear **antecedent** for each pronoun. That is, the writer needed to mention the *nouns* to which the pronouns refer. In the paragraph above, the writer might have started out like this:

> **Indoor gardening** is an excellent hobby for people with busy and stressful lives.

From now on, every time she uses a pronoun, she should keep in mind what it refers to. Here is how the first two sentences might look:

> **Indoor gardening** is an excellent hobby for people with busy and stressful lives. Moreover, while **it** can provide. . .

On the other hand, she could do something different:

> **Indoor gardening** is an excellent hobby for people with busy and stressful lives. Moreover, while **plants** can provide hours of pleasure and relaxation, **they** do not require a lot of attention.

Use a pronoun only when it has a clear antecedent.

Although pronouns usually refer *back* to their antecedents, they can sometimes refer *forward*. That is, they can sometimes take the place of a noun that appears *later* in the sentence, as in this example:

> While **they** can provide hours of pleasure and relaxation, **plants** do not
> require a lot of attention.

————————————— PRACTICE 1 —————————————

In the paragraph, underline all seven of the pronouns. Then draw an arrow from each pronoun to its antecedent. Don't forget possessive pronouns. The first one has been done for you.

> Indoor gardening is an excellent hobby for people with busy and
> stressful lives. Moreover, while plants can provide hours of pleasure and
> relaxation, they do not require a lot of attention. Daily water and a place in
> the sun are their only requirements. In return, each plant brightens its own
> little corner of the house. Plants do more than just decorate, however.
> Many plant owners report that they feel calmer and more peaceful when
> they water their plants or simply gaze at them.

Answers start on page 181.

Choosing the Correct Pronoun

What is wrong with this sentence?

> An African violet is delicate, so you must water **them** carefully.

Which word is supposed to be the antecedent for *them*? _____ Is the word *violet* singular or plural? _____ Is the pronoun *them* singular or plural? _____

Here there is a problem with *number* in pronoun agreement. The plural pronoun (*them*) does not agree with the singular antecedent (*violet*). To solve the problem, you must change either the pronoun or the antecedent:

> **An African violet** is delicate, so you must water **it** carefully.   OR
> **African violets** are delicate, so you must water **them** carefully.

Here is another problem:

> People who own plants must water them regularly; furthermore, **you** should
>   also give them plant food once a month.

What is the pronoun *you* supposed to refer to? *People*? Remember that the pronoun for *people* should be *they*, not *you*.

This time there is a problem with *person* in pronoun agreement. The antecedent and the pronoun must refer to the same person: *people* and *they*. The problem can be solved two ways:

> **People** who own plants must water them regularly. **They** should also give
>   them plant food once a month.
> Be sure to water **your** plants regularly. **You** should also give them plant
>   food once a month.

One way to avoid confusing pronoun reference is to decide before you write if you want to talk *about* someone (*people, they*) or *to* someone (*you*). Once you have made up your mind, stick to the way you have decided.

Below is a chart illustrating how to make your pronouns agree with their antecedents in number and in person:

Antecedent	Pronouns
you (singular) one person one thing another person or other people and I	you, your, yours, yourself he, she, him, her, etc. it, its, itself we, us, our, ours
you (plural) two or more people or things	you, your, yours, yourselves they, them, their, etc.

———————— PRACTICE 2 ————————

Some of these sentences are correct, and some have errors. If necessary, change the pronouns to agree in number and person with their antecedents. If the sentence is correct, write *OK* in the blank. The first one has been done for you.

_____ 1. Plants bring long-lasting pleasure to ~~its~~ *their* owners.

_____ 2. A cactus requires a lot of sun but little water. Be extremely careful not to overwater them.

_____ 3. Plant owners enjoy just looking at their leafy friends.

_____ 4. My family and I have a virtual jungle in my living room.

_____ 5. If a plant requires bright sun, do not place them in a dark corner of the house.

_____ 6. Children over the age of five can usually be trusted with plant-watering duties. They feel important when they are responsible for their very own plants.

_____ 7. A little boy of seven, for instance, could be taught to take care of their own plant independently.

_____ 8. Some plant lovers actually move to new apartments so that their plants can have better light.

_____ 9. Sometimes plant lovers inadvertently kill one of their green companions. In this situation, you mourn the loss of your plant almost as you would mourn the loss of a beloved pet.

Answers start on page 181.

Tricky Antecedents

Your knowledge of tricky subject-verb agreement can also help you with pronoun agreement. For example, you know from page 121 that words like *each* and *one* are always singular. You also know from page 122 that words like *both* and *many* are always plural.

> **Each** of our daughters has **her** own plant.
> **Both** of the girls take good care of **their** Norfolk Island pines.

Some words can be either singular or plural, depending on the nouns they represent. You learned on page 123 that *all, most,* and *some* are a few of those words.

> **All** of the nuts are in **their** shells.
> **Some** of the meat has lost **its** flavor.

You will recall from page 125 that some nouns are always singular. Be sure to make any pronouns that refer to them singular.

> The evening **news** was unusually long last night; **its** running time was over ninety minutes.

You will also recall from page 126 that some nouns are always plural. Be sure to use the correct plural pronouns in these cases.

> John's **clothes** were dirty, so he changed **them**.

As with subject-verb agreement, using pronouns to refer to collective nouns can sometimes be tricky. As you learned on page 127, when the collective noun is spoken of as a unit, it is singular:

> The softball **team** posed for **its** picture.

But if the individual members are emphasized, it is plural:

> The **committee** disagreed on whether to raise **their** own salaries.

Finally, be careful to use singular and plural pronouns correctly when dealing with a compound antecedent. Can you correct this sentence?

> Shanika or her mother will go get the car. Please go with them.

You are right if you changed *them* to *her*. For a complete discussion of singular and plural compounds, see page 128. You may want to review some of the pages listed before starting the next exercise.

─────────────── PRACTICE 3 ───────────────

Some of these sentences are correct, and some have errors. If necessary, change the pronouns to agree with their antecedents. If the sentence is correct, mark *OK* in the blank. The first one has been done for you.

_____ 1. Some of the plants had lost ~~its~~ their leaves.

_____ 2. Many of the rhododendrons looked unwell. Their leaves were brown and drooping.

_____ 3. My scissors lost its sharpness from cutting off all the dead leaves.

_____ 4. The whole group looked as though it had never seen the light of day.

_____ 5. Each plant had something wrong with their leaves.

_____ **6.** All of the soil needed water right away—they felt bone-dry.

_____ **7.** Neither cactus looks as though they had trouble.

_____ **8.** Most of the plant food was spilled on the floor. It had made quite a mess.

_____ **9.** Either Freddie or Willie forgot to water the plants while I was away. When I find out who it was, I will yell at them.

Answers start on page 181.

A Question of Style

Can you spot the problem in this sentence?

> On the airplane, everyone fastened their seat belt.

Since *everyone* is singular, the plural pronoun *their* should not be used. What should be used instead? While a singular pronoun is required, the exact pronoun to use is a matter of style, not rule.

Even if the sentence applied equally to men and women, the traditional answer was once the following:

> Everyone fastened **his** seat belt.

Today, this usage of a masculine pronoun is often considered sexist. Thus, some people prefer to use both the masculine and feminine pronouns as follows:

> Everyone fastened **his or her** seat belt.   OR
> Everyone fastened **his/her** seat belt.

Still other people find this usage awkward. They avoid the entire issue by using a plural antecedent to start with:

> **All of the passengers** fastened **their** seat belts.

You may want to discuss with your instructor the pros and cons of each alternative. Then choose one style for a piece of writing and stick to it.

CUMULATIVE REVIEW

Show What You Know

Now pull together everything you have learned about pronoun agreement as you do this review exercise.

———————————————— PROOFREAD ————————————————

As the editor of *Green Pinky* magazine for beginning indoor gardeners, you receive the following manuscript to edit.

YOUR JOB: Correct the errors in pronoun agreement.

- In some cases, you will need to change the verb form after you change the pronoun so that the subject and verb agree.
- You will also need to add a word or phrase when you find a pronoun with no antecedent. Use the following words: ~~houseplants~~, ferns, feeding.

In all, thirteen errors will need to be corrected. The first two have been done for you.

               houseplants

Most ~~of them~~ die from incorrect watering. If you neglect to water them

         they

regularly, ~~it~~ will die a rapid death. On the other hand, if he overwaters

them, they will die slowly as they turn yellow and the leaves drop from the

stems.

    How do you know how much water to use? The answer depends in

large part on the plants itself. You need to read enough about each plant to

know how frequently it requires water. If you have a cactus or a succulent,

for example, you should water them very infrequently. However, if you have

them, you may need to water it daily.

    It is another important issue. Determining how much fertilizer a plant

needs can be tricky. The directions on many commercial fertilizers

recommend too frequent feeding, so they'd do best to ignore it. Instead, use

the instructions given by a reputable plant-care book.

    Our next issue will be loaded with news—some of them good and some

of them bad—for plants with pest problems. Learn which plants can be

saved and which must be laid to rest.

Answers start on page 181.

CHAPTER 7
MODIFIERS AND
PARALLEL STRUCTURE

Goals

- To correctly use the words *who, whom, which,* and *that* in adjective clauses
- To place adjective clauses, prepositional phrases, and other modifiers correctly
- To understand when and when not to use commas around modifying phrases
- To construct sentences with parallel structure

ADJECTIVE CLAUSES

People Who Need People

Amateur photographers are people **who take pictures for pleasure**.

A disk camera is a camera **which uses a film disk instead of a cartridge or roll**.

INSIGHT

The sentences above are a special kind of complex sentence. Each contains a main clause and an ***adjective clause*** (in **boldface**). Adjective clauses describe nouns. To see how they do this, go through the following steps:

Amateur photographers are people . . .
What *kind* of people?
. . . people **who take pictures for pleasure**.

A disk camera is a camera . . .
What *kind* of camera?
. . . a camera _____

Like any clause, an adjective clause has a subject and a verb. See if you can find the *verb* of each adjective clause above. Underline each and label it with *V*.

You are right if you identified *take* and *uses*. Now what are the subjects of these clauses? (Hint: look at the words immediately before the verbs.) _____ and _____ You are right again if you wrote the words *who* and *which*. These are pronouns used in adjective clauses. How do you know when to use *who* and when to use *which*? Look at these examples and see if you can tell.

. . . people who . . .	. . . a camera which . . .
. . . a man who . . .	. . . machines which . . .
. . . women who . . .	. . . a book which . . .
. . . an expert who . . .	. . . things which . . .

The pronoun *who* is used for _____, and the pronoun *which* is used for _____. If you saw that *who* is for people and *which* for things, you were absolutely correct. Here is another adjective clause pronoun that can be used for either people *or* things: *that*. The sample sentences could be rewritten as follows:

> Amateur photographers are people **that** take pictures for pleasure.
> A disk camera is a camera **that** uses a film disk instead of a cartridge or roll.

> In adjective clauses, use these subject pronouns:*
> who ———→ people
> that ↗
> which ———→ things

Some Common Problems

Be careful! You learned about collective nouns on page 127: words like *club, organization, company*, and *government*. These words should be treated as things when preceding adjective clauses. Therefore, be sure to use the pronouns *that* or *which* with words of this type.

> WRONG: The company **who** hired me operated a photo lab.
> RIGHT: The company **which** hired me operated a photo lab.
> RIGHT: The company **that** hired me operated a photo lab.

Never use the word *what* as a pronoun in an adjective clause.

> WRONG: He bought a camera **what** had a built-in flash.
> RIGHT: He bought a camera **which** had a built-in flash.
> RIGHT: He bought a camera **that** had a built-in flash.

---

*NOTE TO THE INSTRUCTOR:
Some writers, editors, and teachers feel that it is preferable to use *who* for people and *that* only for things. Others feel that *that* should be used for restrictive (identifying) clauses and *which* should be used only for nonrestrictive clauses set off by commas. Both these matters are open to much debate, and grammar handbooks and textbooks offer different guidelines. Feel free to add qualifying comments to this lesson if you subscribe to either view.

──────── PRACTICE ────────

Each sentence below uses the pronoun *that*. Rewrite each sentence using *who* or *which* correctly. The first one has been done for you.

1. Amateur photographers are people that take pictures for pleasure.

   Amateur photographers are people who take pictures for pleasure.

2. Professional photographers are people that earn money for their camera work.

3. A camera that develops its own photos is called a self-developer.

4. Photographers that work in portrait studios earn a steady income.

5. The room that is used to develop photographs is called a darkroom.

6. There are a number of magazines that specialize in photography.

7. Professionals and amateurs that buy these magazines can improve their techniques.

8. Some amateurs join clubs that encourage members to share new photography techniques.

Answers start on page 182.

WHO AND WHOM

For Whom the Bell Tolls

1. The photographer **who** covered the banquet was excellent.
2. The photographer **whom** the company hired was excellent.

INSIGHT

Why does sentence 2 use the pronoun *whom* instead of *who*? To find out, underline the adjective clause in sentence 1. In this clause, the verb is the word _____. As you learned on page 140, the subject of the clause is *who*:

$$ \text{S} \quad \text{V}$$
The photographer (who covered the banquet) was excellent.

Now underline the adjective clause in sentence 2. In this clause the verb is the word _____. The subject of the clause is *the company*. (The company did the hiring.) So what is *whom*, if it's not the subject? It's the *object*:

$$ \text{O} \qquad \text{S} \quad \text{V}$$
The photographer (whom the company hired) was excellent.

Here is an easy way to understand:

1. The photographer was excellent.
   He covered the banquet.
   The photographer **who** covered the banquet was excellent.

2. The photographer was excellent.
   The company hired **him**.
   The photographer **whom** the company hired was excellent.

The pronoun *whom* is used when the *object* of an adjective clause is a person or people.

> **Use the pronoun *whom* when it is the object of an adjective clause. Use it for people only.**

Must *whom* always be used as the object? No. The pronoun *that* can be used instead:

The photographer **that** the company hired was excellent.

—————————— PRACTICE 1 ——————————

Complete the sentences using *who* and *whom* correctly. Remember to use *who* as the subject and *whom* as the object.

1. The photographer _____ the company hired was excellent.
2. The chef _____ prepared the meal was superb.
3. The guests _____ the company invited were longtime clients.
4. The man _____ the company honored with the award bowed gracefully.
5. The woman _____ presented the award gave a speech honoring the recipient.

Answers start on page 182.

—————————— PRACTICE 2 ——————————

Copy and complete these sentences. The first two have been done for you.

1. This is the woman whom . . .
   This is the woman whom the company honored recently.

2. This is the woman who . . .
   This is the woman who increased productivity in her department.

3. That is the gentleman whom . . .
4. That is the gentleman who . . .
5. Here is the telephone number of an attorney whom . . .
6. Here is the telephone number of an attorney who . . .
7. Here is how you can reach the doctor who . . .
8. This is the doctor to whom . . .

Answers will vary.

PLACEMENT OF ADJECTIVE CLAUSES

The Man Who Knew Too Much

Can you spot a problem in one of these two sentences?

> **1.** The woman **who knew CPR** saved Mr. Hailey's life.
> **2.** The woman saved Mr. Hailey's life **who knew CPR**.

INSIGHT

Both sentences contain the adjective clause *who knew CPR*. However, in one sentence this clause appears in the wrong place. Which sentence do you think is right, 1 or 2? _____ If you said that sentence 1 is correct, you are right. What makes sentence 2 wrong?

Remember that adjective clauses *describe*, or modify, nouns. Which noun does the adjective clause *who knew CPR* modify—*woman* or *life*? _____ You're right if you said it modifies *woman*, not *life*. (*Which* woman saved Mr. Hailey's life? It was the woman *who knew CPR*.) Therefore, the adjective clause belongs right after the word *woman*. It is incorrect—and confusing—to put it anywhere else in the sentence. In sentence 2, the clause appears after the word *life*—making it look as though Mr. Hailey's life knew CPR!

Of course, adjective clauses can appear in the middle or at the end of the sentence, depending on the location of the noun being modified. Compare these two correct sentences:

> The woman **who knew CPR** saved Mr. Hailey's life.

> Mr. Hailey's life was saved by the woman **who knew CPR**.

> **Always put the adjective clause *immediately after* the noun it modifies.**

PRACTICE

Rewrite each sentence, adding the adjective clause in parentheses. The first one has been done for you.

1. The woman hurried to the scene of the accident. (*who knew CPR*)

   The woman who knew CPR hurried to the scene of the accident.

2. The man was very lucky to have survived. (*who had the heart attack*)

3. The stricken man was surrounded by people. (*who watched helplessly*)

4. Someone remembered that he had a friend and hurried to find her. (*who knew CPR*)

5. The woman had just been trained in CPR the week before. (*who saved the man's life*)

6. The ambulance had been stuck in a traffic jam. (*that finally arrived on the scene*)

7. The ambulance took the man to a hospital, and an emergency team went to work on him right away. (*that was located only blocks away*)

Answers start on page 182.

SUBJECT-VERB AGREEMENT IN ADJECTIVE CLAUSES

He Who Sees Everything

Which verb is correct: *complain* or *complains*?

1. He is a worker who _____ about everything.
2. They are workers who _____ about everything.

INSIGHT

Which is the correct verb form to use in each sentence? The subject pronoun alone (*who*) could be either singular or plural. You need to look back to the noun it modifies. In sentence 1, which noun is being modified? _____ How about sentence 2? _____ In sentence 1, *who* refers to the singular noun *worker*, and in sentence 2, *who* refers to the plural noun *workers*. Here is how the corrected sentences should look:

1. He is a worker who **complains** about everything.
2. They are workers who **complain** about everything.

> **To make sure your verbs agree with their subjects in adjective clauses, look back to the noun being modified.**

—————————— PRACTICE ——————————

Copy and complete each sentence. Check your subject-verb agreement. The first one has been done for you.

1. A whiner is a person who . . .

   A whiner is a person who complains about everything.

2. A bad sport is a person who . . .

3. They are good parents who . . .

4. A good camera is one that . . .

5. Potato chips are the sort of junk food which . . .

6. Fast-food restaurants are places which . . .

7. McDonald's is a restaurant that . . .

8. My doctor is a physician who . . .

Answers will vary.

REVIEW

Adjective Clauses

Pull together all you know about adjective clauses as you do this review exercise.

──────────────── PROOFREAD ────────────────

As the head of the security system for Second National Bank, you must submit a weekly report to the bank president detailing all points related to the bank's security. As you are very busy, you usually write the reports in a hurry, and you need to spend extra time proofreading them carefully before you submit them.

YOUR JOB: Find and correct the ten errors with adjective clauses. You may have to change a pronoun or move an adjective clause to a different position in the sentence.

Monday, March 28

Security Guard Mendoza reported a suspicious finding in the safe-deposit area. She saw a safe-deposit box what had been left open. Moments later, the bank patron returned who was renting the box and explained that he had had to step out for a moment to use the restroom.

Wednesday, March 30

Security Guard Fredriks was approached by a woman which said she had just been robbed of ten dollars after using the automatic teller machine. Upon questioning, the woman revealed that it was her husband what had taken the money. She was afraid he intended to buy cigarettes with the money and wanted the guard to prevent him. Fredriks said he could do nothing. The woman shouted a few words and marched out which I do not care to print.

Friday, April 1

Security Guard Fredriks reported an incident who aroused his suspicion. He saw a man enter the bank who seemed to be wearing a disguise. The man, in fact, was dressed as an old woman, and in his coat pocket there was a large bulge who appeared to be a gun. Fredriks approached the man and asked him to show the contents of the pocket. The man took out a large sweet potato what had sprouts growing from it and offered it to Fredriks. Fredriks said he was about to contact the supervisor which had just come on duty when the man said, "Look at the date, fool!" and ran out of the bank.

Answers start on page 182.

PROBLEMS WITH PREPOSITIONAL PHRASES

In the Laundromat

You have learned that adjectives and adverbs can tell more about nouns and verbs. Phrases can do the same thing. See if you can find a problem with the following sentence:

In the washing machine, Lucy opened the lid and checked the clothes.

INSIGHT

This sentence sounds as though Lucy is in the washing machine! The problem is that the phrase *in the washing machine* is in the wrong place. *In the washing machine* is a **prepositional phrase**, a phrase that begins with a preposition (*in*). A prepositional phrase can describe a noun or a verb, just as adjectives and adverbs do.

To discover how to fix the sentence, you first need to decide where the phrase belongs. That is, what does the phrase *in the washing machine* describe? _____ You were right if you said *clothes*. To fix the sentence, move the phrase close to the word it describes:

Lucy opened the lid and checked the clothes **in the washing machine**.

Put a prepositional phrase close to the word it modifies.

Look at another example:

Ricky and Lucy talked about taking a vacation in the laundromat.

Taking a vacation in the laundromat? Ricky and Lucy must have a *lot* of laundry to do if they intend to spend their week off washing clothes!

What were Lucy and Ricky doing *in the laundromat*? _____ You're right if you said *talking*. To make the sentence clear, move the phrase *in the laundromat* closer to the verb *talked*. In this particular sentence, there are two places where the phrase could be moved:

In the laundromat, Lucy and Ricky talked about taking a vacation.
Lucy and Ricky talked **in the laundromat** about taking a vacation.

———————————— PRACTICE ————————————

Rewrite each sentence correctly, moving the prepositional phrase to the correct place in the sentence. Watch your punctuation. The first one has been done for you.

1. Against the wall, Ricky stared at the long row of dryers.

   Ricky stared at the long row of dryers against the wall.

2. In the cup, Lucy carefully measured out the bleach.

3. On most of the dryers, Ricky was annoyed to find "out of order" signs.

4. In the basket, they began to fold the wet clothes.

5. The attendant refused to give them any change behind the counter.

6. The attendant asked Ricky not to smoke his cigar in an unpleasant voice.

Answers start on page 182.

PROBLEMS WITH OTHER MODIFYING PHRASES

Staying Close

Do you notice anything strange about these sentences?

> Kicking and screaming, I picked up the infant.
> Wet and hungry, I changed and fed the baby.

INSIGHT

Wait a minute. Who is kicking and screaming, wet and hungry—the baby or the writer? We *assume* that the writer is talking about the baby; however, these sentences communicate just the opposite! Once again, the modifying phrases have been misplaced. Now look at the *correct* use of the modifying phrases:

> I picked up the **kicking and screaming** infant.
> I changed and fed the **wet and hungry** baby.

This time, all of the phrases appear next to the nouns they modify. Go back to the correct sentences and underline the nouns that are being modified. If you underlined *infant* and *baby*, you were right.

Now examine the modifying phrases themselves. The first sentence uses *ing* forms (*Kicking and screaming*) and the second uses adjectives (*Wet and hungry*). Past participles can also be used as parts of modifying phrases, as in this sentence:

> **Shaken by the sound of the phone ringing**, the baby began to scream again.

> **Modifying phrases can contain *ing* phrases, adjectives or adverbs, or past participles.
> Modifying phrases must appear close to the words they modify.**

—————————— PRACTICE ——————————

Each of these sentences has a misplaced modifying phrase. Rewrite the sentence, moving the phrase so that it is correctly close to the word or words it modifies. The first one has been done for you.

1. Kicking and screaming, I had to attend to the baby.
   <u>I had to attend to the kicking and screaming baby.</u>

2. I almost called the doctor, worried about the baby.

3. Struggling against me, I tried to lift the infant.

4. Sitting on a tall shelf, he cried for his teddy bear.

5. His mother saw him striding into the room.

6. He put his arms around her neck reaching for her.

7. Now sleeping soundly, she smiled at the baby.

Answers start on page 183.

DANGLING MODIFIERS

The Dangling Conversation

How would you fix the following problem sentence?

Crying lustily, I dashed to his crib.

INSIGHT

This sentence contains a problem with a modifier. The modifier, of course, is *crying lustily*. Can it be moved to a different part of the sentence?

??   I dashed to his **crying lustily** crib.   ??

The problem is that probably a baby is crying lustily, but there is no baby mentioned. *Crying lustily* in this sentence is a ***dangling modifier***, a modifier dangling by itself with no word to describe. Sentences with dangling modifiers need to be rewritten entirely:

The baby was crying lustily, **so** I dashed to his crib.
As the baby continued to cry lustily, I dashed to his crib.
The baby's lusty cries made me dash to his crib.

These are but a few ways the sentence can be rewritten. As you have seen, the writer can choose a compound sentence, a complex sentence, or a different simple sentence.

> **Sentences with dangling modifiers need to be rewritten
> to include the word or words being modified.**

Try another example.

After defending myself successfully, the attacker turned and fled.

What is the dangling modifier here? _____
You're right if you said *after defending myself successfully*. What word or words should this phrase be modifying? _____ You're right again if you said the word *I* or *me*. Here are some ways the sentence could be rewritten:

After **I defended** myself successfully, the attacker turned and fled.
I defended myself successfully, **so** the attacker turned and fled.
After defending myself successfully, **I watched the attacker turn and flee**.

─────── PRACTICE ───────

The following sentences about the witnessing of a crime all use modifying phrases incorrectly. Rewrite each sentence using a compound sentence, a complex sentence, or a different simple sentence. In each case, different solutions are possible. The first one has been done for you.

1. Looking out the window, the man on the street ran up behind the woman.

   <u>Looking out the window, I saw the man on the</u>
   <u>street run up behind the woman.</u>

2. Screaming for help, he grabbed her purse and ran.

3. Running down the street, I picked up the telephone and dialed the police.

4. Back at the window again, the woman had jumped up and was chasing her attacker.

5. Amazed at the woman's speed, she caught up with the man.

6. Grabbing him by the hood of his jacket, he lost his balance.

7. Falling to the ground, the woman kicked the startled man.

8. Standing menacingly above him, the man shielded his head and begged for mercy.

9. Victorious, the man yielded up the stolen pocketbook.

Answers start on page 183.

USING COMMAS WITH MODIFIERS

Making the Identification

1. Judge Howard had accepted bribes and payoffs.
2. Judge Howard, a respected man in the community, had accepted bribes and payoffs.
3. Judge Howard, who had once been a respected man in the community, had accepted bribes and payoffs.

INSIGHT

Each sentence above has the same subject, *Judge Howard*. Sentences 2 and 3, however, have a modifier between the subject and the verb. Why do commas appear around the modifier?

First answer these questions. *Who* is the sentence about? _____ By the time you get to the modifier, do you need it to *identify* the person being talked about, or do you *already* know who he is? _____

The modifier does *not* identify the person—you already know that the sentence is about Judge Howard! The modifier simply provides some interesting extra information about this man. The commas indicate that the information is extra information—not information that is needed to identify the person.

Look at the sentence below:

> The grand jury indicted Judge Howard, once a respected man in the community.

In this sentence, only one comma is used because the modifier appears at the end of the sentence.

────────────────── PRACTICE 1 ──────────────────

Add the modifier in parentheses after the correct noun in each sentence. Add a comma or commas as necessary. The first two have been done for you.

1. Judge Howard had accepted bribes and payoffs. (*once a respected man in the community*)

   Judge Howard, once a respected man in the community,
   had accepted bribes and payoffs.

2. The newspapers vilified Judge Howard. (*once a respected man in the community*)

   The newspapers vilified Judge Howard, once a respected
   man in the community.

3. The Cedar Valley *News* published a scathing editorial against him. (*which had previously endorsed the judge*)

4. The judge was supported only by the *Midnight Mind*. (*a local scandal sheet*)

5. The *Midnight Mind* had reportedly accepted money from the judge. (*not known for its journalistic excellence*)

6. The town's only high school took down the judge's picture. (*which the judge had attended in his youth*)

7. The judge was the butt of several jokes on "Komedy Tonite." (*a comedy show on the local cable station*)

Answers start on page 183.

When to Use Commas

1. The judge who had once won three integrity medals in a row was indicted on corruption charges.
2. Judge Howard, who had once won three integrity medals in a row, was indicted on corruption charges.

INSIGHT

The sentences above both have modifying clauses that tell more about the judge. Sentence 2 is the type of modifier you have just been studying, a nonidentifying clause. You already know the sentence is about Judge Howard; the clause *who had once won three integrity medals in a row* just tells a bit more about him.

Now look at sentence 1. What is the subject of this sentence? the _____

You're right if you said *the judge*. Out of all the judges around, which one is being discussed here? the one _____

You're right if you said *the one who had once won three integrity medals in a row*. The modifier in sentence 1 is an ***identifying modifier*** that is necessary to help the reader identify which judge is being talked about.

How do you know when and when not to use commas in your own writing? Read through the following examples and explanations.

Words needed to identify noun—no commas

The lawyer seated on the right spoke forcefully and convincingly.

Which lawyer did you say? The one seated on the left? No! The lawyer seated on the right . . . . The phrase *identifies* the noun.

Words not needed to identify noun—commas

Judge Howard's lawyer, who was seated on the right, spoke forcefully and convincingly.

Right from the start, you know the sentence is about Judge Howard's lawyer. The modifier simply lets you know where he was sitting—it doesn't identify the noun.

> **Use commas only when the extra words are not needed to identify the noun.**

The pronoun *that* can appear only in identifying clauses. Therefore, commas must *never* be used around an adjective clause starting with *that*.

> WRONG: The newspaper, that I usually buy, supported the judge.
> RIGHT: The newspaper that I usually buy supported the judge.

———————————— PRACTICE 2 ————————————

Each sentence contains a phrase or clause that modifies a noun. The noun being modified is in **boldface**. Add commas only where the phrase or clause is *not* needed to identify the noun. If no comma is needed, write *OK* in the blank. The first two have been done for you.

_OK_   1. **The lawyer** who defended Judge Howard had an impeccable record.

———   2. **Harvey Whiteglove** who represented the judge in court had a "Mr. Clean" reputation.

———   3. **Bribery** a very serious crime cannot be tolerated in our judicial system.

———   4. **Martin Lawless** an attorney long suspected of corruption was one of many participants in the scheme.

———   5. **The bribes** paid by Martin Lawless amounted to nearly ten thousand dollars.

———   6. Judge Howard received **a ten-year sentence** a stiff and unforgiving penalty.

———   7. The penalty was a warning to all other **judges** that have participated in the payoff network.

———   8. Judge Howard will serve his time at **a prison** located near the southern border of the state.

———   9. **Halsted Penitentiary** located near the southern border of the state will be the judge's new home.

———   10. We need to renew our faith in **the judicial system** a system based on honesty and trust.

─────────────── **PROOFREAD** ───────────────

As the editor of the Cedar Valley *News*, you must work on the following editorial about Judge Howard.

Your job: Add and subtract commas as necessary. You will need to add a total of eight commas and subtract a total of eleven.

Judge Howard once a respected community leader has been found guilty of corruption. The trial, that he received, was a fair one, and the evidence, presented at the trial, was overwhelming. Judge Howard has undermined our faith in the judicial system a system, in which we all must trust. What motivated Judge Howard? Was his salary which had just risen to $50,000 insufficient? Was his need for a car, with reclining leather seats and a wet bar, undeniable? We think not. Judge Howard was motivated by greed the ugliest of sins. Any judge, who is motivated by greed, cannot be an upholder of justice. We applaud the decision, made by the court. We applaud the sentence, received by the judge. And we applaud Cedar Valley a community of decent and hardworking people for its adherence to the highest standards of honesty and justice.

Answers start on page 183.

PARALLEL STRUCTURE

Keeping Each Line Straight

Compare these two sentences:

1. Finding a good job, earning a good salary, and to save money are my goals.
2. Finding a good job, earning a good salary, and saving money are my goals.

INSIGHT

Which sentence is correctly written, 1 or 2? _____ If you selected sentence 2, you were right. Both sentences contain compound subjects. However, the elements in the compound subject of sentence 1 are not parallel: two *ing* words (*finding* and *earning*) are mixed in with *to save*. The elements of the compound in sentence 2 *are* parallel: three *ing* words (*finding, earning,* and *saving*).

When a sentence has **parallel structure**, the elements of a compound subject, verb, or complement are in the same form. Try another parallel puzzle:

I am living, work, and studying in the city of Boise.

This sentence has a compound verb. Is the structure parallel? _____ You're right if you said no. The sentence mixes the present continuous (*am living* and *studying*) with the simple present (*work*). There are two ways the sentence can be fixed:

I am living, **working**, and studying in the city of Boise.
I **live**, work, and **study** in the city of Boise.

Let's turn now to a slightly different parallel problem. Which of the two sentences below is incorrect?

1. Giles bought a Mercedes, a Porsche, and a BMW.
2. Giles bought a Mercedes, a Porsche, a BMW, and enjoyed flaunting them all.

If you said sentence 2, you're correct. Why? Let's take a close look at the elements of each of the compound complements. First, take another look at sentence 1:

Giles bought a <u>Mercedes</u>, a <u>Porsche</u>, and a <u>BMW</u>.
                   (noun)   *(noun)*   *(noun)*

As you can see, each of the three elements in the compound complement are nouns—proper nouns in this case. Now take a look at sentence 2:

Giles bought a <u>Mercedes</u>, a <u>Porsche</u>, a <u>BMW</u>, and <u>enjoyed</u> flaunting them all.
                   (noun)   *(noun)*   *(noun)*   *(verb)*

Are all the elements parallel? No! One of them begins with a verb (*enjoyed*), and three begin with a noun (*Mercedes, Porsche,* and *BMW.*)

How could the sentence be fixed? The simplest way is to split up those two verbs and make two sentences:

Giles bought a Mercedes, a Porsche, **and** a BMW. **He** enjoyed flaunting them all.

Use parallel structure for compound subjects, verbs, and complements.	

─────────────────────── **PRACTICE 1** ───────────────────────

Read each sentence carefully. If it uses parallel structure, write *OK* in the blank. If it does not use parallel structure, rewrite it correctly. There are usually several ways to rewrite a nonparallel sentence. The first one has been done for you.

_____ 1. My job pays poorly and no benefits.

<u>My job pays poorly and provides no benefits.</u>

_____ 2. Paying the rent and the bills can be difficult.

_____ 3. I often fantasize about being rich and buy a Mercedes.

_____ 4. A Mercedes is a luxury car, a status symbol, and sends a message about its owner.

_____ 5. Owning it and driving it around the city would make me feel proud.

_____ 6. Unfortunately, I can't afford to buy or the maintenance of even a Yugo.

_____ 7. A new job with better benefits and well paying must be my first priority.

_____ 8. I have experience, expertise, and deserve a position in a good company.

_____ 9. I must start to look through the want ads and write letters to companies with interesting job offers.

_____ 10. Perhaps I will never be able to buy or driving a Mercedes.

_____ 11. However, a small car and earning a decent income are realistic goals for me.

Answers start on page 184.

Parallel Structure with Phrases and Clauses

Here is a different kind of parallel problem:

> Mr. Smith told the court what his name was, his current address, and what he did for a living.

Underline the three elements of the compound complement. Now examine each group, keeping in mind that a clause is a group of words containing a subject and a complete verb and that a phrase is a group of words *without* this combination. Is *what his name was* a phrase or a clause? _____ How about *his current address*? _____ How about *what he did for a living*? _____ Does this sentence use parallel structure? _____

You're right if you saw that this sentence does *not* use parallel structure. In its compound complement, it mixes a phrase (*his current address*) with two clauses (*what his name was, what he did for a living*). For parallel structure, this sentence could be rewritten in several ways:

Using Clauses

> Mr. Smith told the court what his name was, **where he lived**, and what he did for a living.

Using Phrases

> Mr. Smith told the court **his name**, his current address, and **his occupation**.

Two Separate Sentences

Mr. Smith gave the court **his name** and his current address. He also told the court **what he did for a living**.

Modifying phrases and clauses can also be compound, and, as a result, a sentence can have problems with parallel structure. Study the following problem and several possible solutions:

PROBLEM: Ms. Tubbs is a teacher with a pleasant voice and who has a warm personality.

SOLUTION: Ms. Tubbs is a teacher **with a pleasant voice** and **a warm personality**.

SOLUTION: Ms. Tubbs is a teacher **who has a pleasant voice** and **a warm personality**.

Use parallel structure for phrases and clauses.

─────────── **PRACTICE 2** ───────────

Each sentence below has a problem with parallel structure. Rewrite the sentence to solve the problem. There may be more than one way to do this. The first one has been done for you.

1. The lawyer was a woman with a sharp mind and who made shrewd decisions.

   The lawyer was a woman who had a sharp mind and who made shrewd decisions.

2. She wanted to know our names, where we lived, and our phone numbers.

3. She also requested to know where we worked and our schedules.

4. We were people who knew nothing of the law and with an ingrained mistrust of the legal profession.

5. The lawyer was quite expensive but who proved very competent.

6. We were satisfied with her handling of our case and what the outcome of the trial was.

Answers start on page 184.

CUMULATIVE REVIEW

Show What You Know

Write a three-paragraph composition of six to eight sentences in each paragraph. Choose one of the following topics.

1. Types of bosses

You may have worked under several different bosses in your life. Think about their different personalities and managing styles. Can you classify them into different types? Write a composition describing two or three types and giving real-life examples.

2. Types of mothers/types of fathers

In your life, you have surely observed many kinds of parents. Think about their different personalities and child-rearing styles. Can you classify them into different types? Write a composition describing two or three types and giving real-life examples.

3. Types of cars

If you are interested in cars, you know there are many different types. Write a composition describing two or three different types and giving examples.

4. Types of sports

If you are an athlete or a sports fan, you know there are many different sports. Can you classify them into different types? Write a composition describing two or three different types and giving examples and explanations.

A composition of this type will take some thinking and planning. It would be wise to make an outline or at least jot down some notes before you begin. When you write, use adjective clauses and other kinds of modifying phrases and clauses.

When you are finished writing, proofread your work.

☑ Make sure you have used an interesting variety of sentence lengths and types (simple, compound, and complex).
☑ Make sure that you have used adjective clauses and other modifying phrases and clauses correctly.
☑ Make sure that all compound elements use parallel structure.
☑ Make sure that all verbs agree with subjects.

FINAL TEST

This test covers the main topics you have studied in this book. There are 100 points in all. There is no time limit on this test. After you have finished, check your answers on pages 164–165. The evaluation chart on page 166 will tell you in which areas you need to do additional work.

PART 1: FINDING AND FIXING SENTENCE PROBLEMS (19 points)

Some of the sentences below are correct, and some are not.

- By each sentence, write *OK*, *FRAG* (for fragment), or *RUN-ON*.
- Now rewrite the fragments and run-ons from above to make correct, complete sentences. Use a separate sheet of paper. You will need to add new words or clauses to fix the sentences.

Two examples have been done for you below.

EXAMPLES: ___OK___ **a.** There was an accident at the plant not long ago.

___FRAG___ **b.** A terrible accident.

_____It was a terrible accident._____

_____ **1.** While most of the workers were taking their coffee break, a gas tank exploded.

_____ **2.** Because someone had left a burning cigarette near the tank.

_____ **3.** The explosion occurred, people screamed and panicked.

_____ **4.** Running for the doors.

_____ **5.** A foreman came and calmed the people down.

_____ **6.** One person was hurt.

_____ **7.** The person who had been smoking the cigarette.

_____ **8.** He suffered severe burns, he was very lucky to survive.

_____ **9.** Also, hearing damage.

_____ **10.** He stayed in the hospital for several months he was finally released.

_____ **11.** Back at work now.

PART 2: VERBS (11 points)

Write the correct form of the verb in parentheses. Think carefully about the meaning and the tense. Write a negative if indicated.

When Sandra Soto _____ for a job with the city sanitation
                 1. (apply)

department ten years ago, she was told by the personnel office that women

could not serve as sanitation engineers. Ms. Soto _____ that
                              2. (know)

she _____ as strong as any man, however. A few years earlier,
  3. (be)

she _____ a job because of her gender, and she _____ to
  4. (lose)   **5. (intend—negative)**

miss another opportunity this time. She took her case to court.

After an extended court battle, the city was forced to hire Ms. Soto. So far, she _____ as a sanitation engineer for five years, and
6. (*work*)
she _____ her ability many times over. Her
7. (*prove*)
job _____ an easy one. She _____ to ride outside of a
8. (*be*—negative)   9. (*have*)
truck and lift heavy garbage cans. She _____, though.
10. (*mind*—negative)
The pay and benefits are excellent. When she retires, she _____ a
11. (*receive*)
good, solid pension, too. For Sandra Soto, the struggle has been worth the effort.

PART 3: SUBJECT-VERB AGREEMENT, PRONOUN AGREEMENT, NOUNS, ADJECTIVES, ADVERBS (20 points)

Circle the correct word or phrase for each blank in the paragraph.

Finding new jobs for older workers is the goal of ElderWork, Inc. When older (*people/peoples*) lose (*his or her/their*) jobs, it is often
1   2
(*real hard/really hard*) to find another company willing to hire (*you/them*).
3   4
ElderWork, one of this (*city's/cities*) many not-for-profit corporations,
5
(*attempts/attempt*) to solve this problem through an extensive search for
6
(*company's/companies*) willing to hire older workers.
7

Though the companies ElderWork contacts are often enthusiastic about the idea, many of the top personnel (*is/are*) unwilling to make a
8
commitment. Most company representatives are unwilling to appear prejudiced against the aged but are (*equal/equally*) leery of making any
9
guarantees. A spokeswoman for ElderWork says that a worker who (*has/have*) kept up with (*his or her/their*) field (*is/are*) usually the easiest
10   11   12
to place. According to this spokeswoman, an older worker with (*a number of/a great deal of*) experience is about as easy to place as a
13
relatively inexperienced younger one.

ElderWork does not discriminate against everyone who (*looks/look*)
14
(*youthful/youthfully*), however. (*It has/They have*) a subsidiary called
15   16
YouthWork to find jobs for teenagers and young adults.

Simple economics often (*works/work*) in the older and younger
17
workers' favor. A teenager or an older worker often (*accepts/accept*) more
18
modest wages than a middle-aged one. There (*is/are*) another reason why
19

older or younger workers may be attractive prospects to employers. One

manager reports that his team of teenagers and senior citizens

(*completes/complete*) the tasks assigned with great diligence and pride.
   20

PART 4: PUNCTUATION (15 points)

Add commas, quotation marks, or semicolons as needed to the sentences below. Some sentences do not need any marks added.

1. Robert Johnson a personnel manager at a large bank is a volunteer coach for the Livingston Youth Center.

2. He helps the children develop physical strength responsibility and pride.

3. The children respect Mr. Johnson and have fun with him, too.

4. In a recent interview Mr. Johnson said I earn more money at my bank job but this job gives me just as much satisfaction.

5. Mr. Johnson also said that the children were more enthusiastic than many of his employees.

6. Even though Mr. Johnson has little free time he is pleased to spend it at the youth center.

7. He volunteered to become a coach because he wanted to help out in the community.

8. He loves children and sports so he volunteered to become coach.

9. He loves children and sports therefore he volunteered to become coach.

PART 5: PRONOUNS, CONTRACTIONS, AND PROPER NOUNS (14 points)

Read the passage and look for mistakes in pronouns, contractions, and the use of capital and small letters. Cross out any errors and write the correct word above.

Dear Mrs. Stensweiller,

     This is a note to inform you that you're dog has been in our bushes

again. Its time to demand serious action. You and your husband must take

it upon yourself to keep the dog in the yard. Those bushes of our's are very

delicate and should not be disturbed.

     If this happens again, my wife and me will be forced to call the

Authorities. As you know, this town of platteville, wisconsin, has a Leash

Law. That animal of your's needs a good, strong leash around it's neck.

Perhaps your Veterinarian can recommend one. If there is something you

need to discuss, please call Miranda or myself.

                            Jake McCarthy

PART 6: NEGATIVE, CONDITIONAL, AND MISPLACED AND DANGLING MODIFIERS (13 points)

Read the passage and look for errors in negatives, conditional, and misplaced or dangling modifiers. You may need to cross out errors and write the correct words above, move phrases or clauses to different parts of the sentence, or add words.

Smoking a cigarette, it was a dark and stormy night. The notorious gangster stubbed out his cigarette, who was named John Vicious. Mr. Vicious didn't do nothing the legal way, and now he had escaped from jail. If the guards had been able to stop him, they would of killed him. Shiny and metallic, he polished his gun.

"I ain't had no breaks in this life," he thought. "If I was like my brother Sandy, I would be a podiatrist now. I would have been somebody important if only I had listened to my mother."

Suddenly the hideout was surrounded by police. There was no escape. Booming through the windows, he heard his mother's voice.

"You ain't going anywhere!" she shouted. "A big baby is what you are who should have listened to his mother. You're not smart enough to be no podiatrist. Now stop acting like such a bully!"

Hands in the air, the gun clattered to the floor. "Aw, come on, Mom!" he wailed. "You never let a guy have any fun."

PART 7: ADJECTIVE CLAUSES AND PARALLEL STRUCTURE (8 points)

Read the passage and look for errors in adjective clauses and parallel structure. Cross out any errors and write the correct words above.

The newspaper who reported the fruit-and-vegetable bribery scandal uncovered a number of interesting facts. Apparently the kickbacks went to wholesalers, truck drivers, and to silence the police. The reporter which unearthed the scandal had gone undercover for several months. He had posed as a small retailer whom was trying to get into the business. Thus, he learned who the corrupt dealers were, their methods, and how they forced noncomplying stores to buy rotten produce. For example, he once had to accept a shipment of bruised tomatoes, black bananas, and that the peaches went bad. The wholesalers who he had paid for this shipment refused to give him a refund. Because of this reporter's work, the newspaper was able to provide an important service to the public, honest retailers, and helped the authorities.

Answers start on page 164.

FINAL TEST ANSWER KEY

Part 1: Finding and Fixing Sentence Problems

You may have fixed the fragments and run-ons in a different way. Have your instructor or a friend check your work.

1. *OK*
2. *FRAG*   The explosion occurred because someone had left a burning cigarette near the tank.
3. *RUN-ON*   When the explosion occurred, people screamed and panicked.
4. *FRAG*   They were running for the doors.
5. OK
6. OK
7. *FRAG*   The person who had been smoking the cigarette was the only one hurt.
8. *RUN-ON*   He suffered severe burns; therefore, he was very lucky to survive.
9. *FRAG*   Also, he suffered hearing damage.
10. *RUN-ON*   After he stayed in the hospital for several months, he was finally released.
11. *FRAG*   He is back at work now.

Part 2: Verbs

1. applied
2. knew
3. was
4. had lost
5. did not intend
6. has worked
7. has proven or has proved
8. is not
9. has
10. doesn't mind
11. will receive

Part 3: Subject-Verb Agreement, Pronoun Agreement, Nouns, Adjectives, Adverbs

1. people
2. their
3. really hard
4. them
5. city's
6. attempts
7. companies
8. are
9. equally
10. has
11. his or her
12. is
13. a great deal of
14. looks
15. youthful
16. It has
17. works
18. accepts
19. is
20. completes

Part 4: Punctuation

1. Robert Johnson [,] a personnel manager at a large bank [,] is a volunteer coach for the Livingston Youth Center.
2. He helps the children develop physical strength [,] responsibility [,] and pride.
3. *no punctuation needed*
4. In a recent interview Mr. Johnson said [,] ["] I earn more money at my bank job [,] but this job gives me just as much satisfaction. ["]
5. *no punctuation needed*
6. Even though Mr. Johnson has little free time [,] he is pleased to spend it at the youth center.
7. *no punctuation needed*
8. He loves children and sports [,] so he volunteered to become coach.
9. He loves children and sports [;] therefore [,] he volunteered to become coach.

Part 5: Pronouns, Contractions, and Proper Nouns

Here is how the corrected paragraph should look.

Dear Mrs. Stensweiller,

    This is a note to inform you that **your** dog
                                        1
has been in our bushes again. **It's** time to
                                    2
demand serious action. You and your husband must take it upon **yourselves** to keep the dog in
                                  3
the yard. Those bushes of **ours** are very delicate
                                 4
and should not be disturbed.

    If this happens again, my wife and **I** will be
                                  5
forced to call the **authorities**. As you know, this
                       6
town of **Platteville, Wisconsin**, has a **leash law**.
            7   8   9   10
That animal of **yours** needs a good, strong leash
           11

164

around **its** neck. Perhaps your **veterinarian** can
 12   13
recommend one. If there is something you need

to discuss, please call Miranda or **me**.
                                      14

Jake McCarthy

Part 6: Negative, Conditional, and Misplaced and Dangling Modifiers

You may have fixed the double negatives and dangling modifiers in a different way. Have your instructor or a friend look over your work.

Smoking a cigarette, **the gangster noticed**
                                          1
that it was a dark and stormy night. The

notorious gangster**, who was named John**
                                         2
Vicious, stubbed out his cigarette. Mr. Vicious

didn't do **anything** the legal way, and now he
          3
had escaped from jail. If the guards had been

able to stop him, they would **have** killed him. He
                                4
polished his **shiny and metallic** gun.
              5

"I **haven't** had **any** breaks in this life," he
    6   7
thought. "If I **were** like my brother Sandy, I
              8
would be a podiatrist now. I would have been

somebody important if only I had listened to my

mother."

Suddenly the hideout was surrounded by

police. There was no escape. He heard his

mother's voice **booming through the windows**.
                                        9
"You **aren't** going anywhere!" she shouted.
      10
"A big baby **who should have listened to his**
                              11
mother is what you are. You're not smart enough

to be **a** podiatrist. Now stop acting like such a
        12
bully!"

Hands in the air, **he let the gun clatter to**
                                            13
the floor. "Aw, come on, Mom!" he wailed. "You

never let a guy have any fun."

Part 7: Adjective Clauses and Parallel Structure

You may have fixed the parallel problems in a different way. Have your instructor or a friend look over your work.

The newspaper **that** (or **which**) reported the
                   1
fruit-and-vegetable bribery scandal uncovered a

number of interesting facts. Apparently the

kickbacks went to wholesalers, truck drivers, and

the police. The reporter **who** unearthed the
    2   3
scandal had gone undercover for several months.

He had posed as a small retailer **who** was trying
                                    4
to get into the business. Thus, he learned who

the corrupt dealers were, **what their methods**
                                              5
were, and how they forced noncomplying stores

to buy rotten produce. For example, he once had

to accept a shipment of bruised tomatoes, black

bananas, and **bad peaches**. The wholesalers
                         6
whom he had paid for this shipment refused to
    7
give him a refund. Because of this reporter's

work, the newspaper was able to provide an

important service to the public, honest retailers,

and the authorities.
          8

Final Test Evaluation Chart

Use the chart below to determine the grammar skills in which you need to do the most review. Write the total number of points for each part of the test, and review the areas where you missed half or more of the questions. Then add up the total number of points to find your final score.

Content Area	Item Number	Review Pages	Points
Part 1			
Sentence problems	1, 2, 3, 4, 5, 6, 7, 8, 9, 10, 11	12–16, 25–29, 49–53	____ / 19
Part 2			
Verb tenses	1, 2, 3, 4, 5, 6, 7, 8, 9, 10, 11	85–102	____ / 11
Part 3			
Nouns	1, 5, 7, 13	58–66	____ / 4
Adjectives and adverbs	3, 9, 15	77–83	____ / 3
Subject-verb agreement	6, 8, 10, 12, 14, 17, 18, 19, 20	118–30	____ / 9
Pronoun agreement	2, 4, 11, 16	133–37	____ / 4
Part 4*			
Comma in a series of three or more	2	22–23, 34–35	____ / 2
Comma in compound sentences	4, 8	33	____ / 2
Comma in complex sentences	6	45	____ / 1
Punctuation in sentences with transition	9	37–40	____ / 2
Punctuation in quoted speech	4	111–116	____ / 3
Comma around nonidentifying phrases	1	152–155	____ / 2
No punctuation needed	3, 5, 7		____ / 3
Part 5**			
Pronouns and contractions	1, 2, 3, 4, 5, 11, 12, 14	67–76	____ / 8
Proper nouns	6, 7, 8, 9, 10, 13	59–60	____ / 6
Part 6**			
Negatives	3, 6, 7, 10, 12	104–107	____ / 5
Conditional	4, 8	108–110	____ / 2
Misplaced and dangling modifiers	1, 2, 5, 9, 11, 13	147–151	____ / 6
Part 7**			
Adjective clauses	1, 3, 4, 7	139–145	____ / 4
Parallel structure	2, 5, 6, 8	156–158	____ / 4
		Total	____ / 100

*In Part 4, score one point for each punctuation mark correctly used. Each sentence where no punctuation mark is needed is also worth one point.

**In Part 5, Part 6, and Part 7, use the answer key on pages 164–165 to find the number for each answer. Score one point for each correct answer.

APPENDIX

Irregular Verbs: Past Forms and Past Participles

The following verbs have the same past form and past participle.

Base Form	Past Form	Past Participle	Base Form	Past Form	Past Participle
bend	bent	bent	lend	lent	lent
bet	bet	bet	lose	lost	lost
bleed	bled	bled	make	made	made
bring	brought	brought	mean	meant	meant
broadcast	broadcast	broadcast	meet	met	met
build	built	built	pay	paid	paid
burst	burst	burst	put	put	put
buy	bought	bought	read	read	read
catch	caught	caught	say	said	said
cost	cost	cost	sell	sold	sold
creep	crept	crept	send	sent	sent
cut	cut	cut	set	set	set
feed	fed	fed	shoot	shot	shot
feel	felt	felt	sit	sat	sat
fight	fought	fought	sleep	slept	slept
find	found	found	spend	spent	spent
flee	fled	fled	spit	spit	spit
grind	ground	ground	split	split	split
have	had	had	stand	stood	stood
hear	heard	heard	sweep	swept	swept
hold	held	held	teach	taught	taught
hurt	hurt	hurt	tell	told	told
keep	kept	kept	think	thought	thought
lay	laid	laid	understand	understood	understood
lead	led	led	wind	wound	wound
leave	left	left			

Past: Yesterday, I... Past participle This month, I have...

The following verb   ples.

Base Form	Past Form	Past Participle
be	was, were	been
bear	bore	borne
become	became	become
begin	began	begun
*bite	bit	bit or bitten
blow	blew	blown
break	broke	broken
choose	chose	chosen
come	came	come
draw	drew	drawn
drink	drank	drunk
drive	drove	driven
eat	ate	eaten
fall	fell	fallen
fly	flew	flown
forget	forgot	forgotten
freeze	froze	frozen
*get	got	got or gotten
give	gave	given
go	went	gone
grow	grew	grown
hide	hid	hidden
know	knew	known
lie	lay	lain
*prove	proved	proved or proven
ride	rode	ridden
ring	rang	rung
run	ran	run
see	saw	seen
*show	showed	showed or shown
sing	sang	sung
speak	spoke	spoken
steal	stole	stolen
swear	swore	sworn
swim	swam	swum
tear	tore	torn
throw	threw	thrown
wear	wore	worn
write	wrote	written

*These verbs have two past participles that are both acceptable.

ANSWER KEY

CHAPTER 1: THE SIMPLE SENTENCE
COMPLETE THAT THOUGHT!
Practice (page 13)

1. NO
2. YES
3. YES
4. NO
5. YES
6. YES
7. NO
8. NO

THE MINIMUM REQUIREMENTS
Practice 1 (page 15)

1. Steven operated the lathe carefully.
2. He added oil regularly.
3. Every evening, Steven worked eight hours at the nail factory.
4. He seemed mature and responsible.
5. His foreman frequently checked the machine.
6. Fortunately, Steven was a careful and conscientious worker.

Practice 2 (page 16)

1. Sara cleaned the gutters on her roof yesterday.
2. To reach them, she climbed a ten-foot ladder.
3. Dead leaves clogged the gutters.
4. Sara thoroughly swept them all away.
5. Unfortunately, she stretched too far to get the corner.
6. Then she suddenly lost her balance.
7. She slipped.

Practice 3 (page 16)

Here is how the sentences should look. We have put each on its own line so that you can see them better.

I dropped out of school at age fourteen.

For years, I did odd jobs around the neighborhood.

I stayed at my parents' house with my younger brothers and sisters.

Eventually, I left.

My income was too small for my own apartment.

As a result, the streets became my home.

Life got more and more difficult.

Fortunately, my cousin kindly took me in.

He found me a job at his factory.

With his encouragement, I returned to school for my GED.

Now I am on my way to better times.

DON'T DO WHAT?
Practice 1 (pages 17-18)

1. I have been living with my cousin for a year.
2. I help him with the rent.
3. He helps me with my schoolwork.
4. I am working at a factory.
5. My cousin has been working there for several years.
6. We will look for new jobs next year.
7. We need more money and more challenge.
8. We have been having a hard time paying bills.

Practice 2 (page 18)

1. You should not skip a month with the electric company.
2. They probably will not be quiet without their money.
3. My cousin does not balance his checkbook.
4. I have not been balancing mine either.
5. With a little luck, we will not be in trouble yet.
6. We do not want our wages garnisheed.

169

Practice 3 (page 19)

1. Where $\underset{HV}{\underline{do}}$ your $\underset{S}{\underline{classes}}$ $\underset{MV}{\underline{meet}}$?
2. How long $\underset{HV}{\underline{do}}$ the $\underset{S}{\underline{classes}}$ $\underset{MV}{\underline{last}}$?
3. $\underset{HV}{\underline{Do}}$ $\underset{S}{\underline{you}}$ $\underset{MV}{\underline{have}}$ different instructors?
4. $\underset{HV}{\underline{Does}}$ your $\underset{S}{\underline{instructor}}$ $\underset{MV}{\underline{meet}}$ with you outside class?
5. What $\underset{HV}{\underline{has}}$ the $\underset{S}{\underline{class}}$ $\underset{HV}{\underline{been}}$ $\underset{MV}{\underline{working}}$ on?
6. $\underset{HV}{\underline{Have}}$ $\underset{S}{\underline{you}}$ $\underset{MV}{\underline{completed}}$ part of the work independently?

Practice 4 (page 20)

1. (you) Ask questions now.
2. statement
3. (you) Read all of the explanations.
4. (you) Do all of the steps outlined.
5. statement
6. (you) Do not cut corners!

BUTCHER, BAKER, CANDLESTICK MAKER
Practice 1 (page 22)

1. CS
2. CV
3. CC
4. CS
5. CC
6. CV

Practice 2 (page 23)

1. Tax hikes are brought up, discussed, and often rejected.
2. State and city governments often need more money for schools, roads, or other projects.
3. no commas needed
4. Candidates, representatives, and the public generally oppose increased taxes.
5. no commas needed
6. Some people write letters, form committees, or use their votes against higher taxes.
7. no commas needed

Practice 3 (page 23)

1. More money is needed for schools, roads, and public transportation.
2. The schools need better facilities, new buildings, and special programs.
3. The buses are expensive but break down frequently.
4. The roads are narrow, bumpy, and full of potholes.
5. Taxes, tolls, or parking fines can pay for roadwork.
6. Community leaders or lawmakers must find solutions to these problems.

Proofread (page 24)

Brett Harper will be your mayor✗and your no-tax advocate. Brett will lower taxes✗and put our city back together. Here is Brett's plan for improving conditions in your schools, your neighborhoods, your homes, and your streets. Brett proposes a volunteer system in the local elementary✗and high schools. Parents✗and local business people will help students with English, science, history, and math in free after-school programs. Brett proposes a workfare program for improvement in neighborhoods✗and homes. People can work for their money by repairing local streets, painting houses, **or** picking up garbage. Brett proposes a crackdown on fines for parking✗and moving violations. Increased fine collection will pay for repairs in roads✗and freeways. Vote for Brett Harper! Brett will get rid of high taxes✗and get our city back in shape!

NOT SAYING ENOUGH
Practice 1 (pages 25-26)

1. frag
2. sent
3. sent
4. frag
5. frag
6. sent
7. frag
8. frag

Practice 2 (pages 26-27)

1. Security is also important. Dogs provide a sense of safety to residents of high-crime areas.
2. Dogs bark and alert their owners to danger. Even small dogs can protect their owners.
3. Unfortunately, they can sometimes disturb neighbors and even family members. Continuous barking can be a real annoyance.
4. Some people are afraid of dogs. A bad experience with one dog can be enough to turn some people against all dogs.

Practice 3 (page 27)

Your answers will probably be different from these. Have your instructor or a friend check over your work to make sure you have fixed the fragments correctly.

1. Dogs can be hard to keep. First, the expense may be too much for people on tight budgets.
2. Dogs bring different benefits to their owners. For one thing, dogs can offer protection to the home.
3. Some relatively small breeds make excellent watchdogs. One example is the bull terrier.
4. Dogs can provide their owners with security. Another benefit is warm and unquestioning affection.

5. Dogs can be highly affectionate. They often show affection by wagging their tails and giving their owners sloppy kisses.

6. Dogs are not for everyone. The lack of freedom for the owner may be a problem for some.

Proofread (page 27)

Your paragraph may look slightly different. Have your instructor or a friend look at your work to make sure you are correcting the fragments correctly.

Dogs and people have been friends **for hundreds of years**. Some benefits of dog ownership are familiar **to everyone**. Others may be less familiar. First, protection **is an important benefit**. Dogs can use their loud barks or their sharp bites to ward off aggressors. Also, **dogs provide** companionship. Dogs keep lonely people company **and give them unquestioning love**. Third, **having a dog can keep the owner in** better health. Studies have shown that dog owners recover more quickly **from heart attacks and strokes than nonowners**. Finally, **dogs can** help with work or daily living. For hundreds of years, sheepdogs **have helped farmers by herding their sheep**. All in all, dogs make excellent protectors, companions, and helpers.

SAYING TOO MUCH
Practice 1 (page 29)

1. sent	5. sent
2. run-on	6. run-on
3. sent	7. run-on
4. run-on	8. run-on

Practice 2 (page 29)

2. The mailman was in a hurry. He didn't watch where he was going.

4. The policeman spotted me. He said I was going ten miles over the speed limit.

6. The mailman was in pain. He began to yell and tried to hit the policeman.

7. The policeman easily grabbed his arm. Then he arrested him.

8. The mailman knew the policeman. He had run off with the mailman's wife many years ago.

SHOW WHAT YOU KNOW
Proofread (page 30)

For a few sentences, different students may have slightly different corrections. Here is one suggestion.

Major league football and baseball are very different. All the baseball teams own minor league teams. Young players go there to acquire their skills. However, National Football League teams draft players right out of college. These players play for the pros right away. There are no lower-level teams for those with less talent.

Professional baseball players have longer careers. Their jobs are less dangerous. They do not have as much physical contact as football players do. Many professional football players have bad knees and need surgery. Furthermore, neck and back injuries are a greater risk for football players.

The average career on a major league baseball team lasts for five years. There is a lot of competition for jobs. Also, a player's skills begin to deteriorate. A pitcher's control can go. Another player's batting average can plummet. It's very risky. No one can guess about the duration of a young player's career.

CHAPTER 2: CONNECTING SENTENCES
I CAN, AND I WILL
Practice 1 (page 33)

1. We got good grades, **but** we couldn't finish school.

2. My parents worked in the fields, **and** I worked with them.

3. We worked long hours every day, **but** we didn't make much money.

4. We didn't earn much, **and** the bills kept piling up.   OR
We didn't earn much, **but** the bills kept piling up.

5. My brothers kept their jobs, **but** I quit.

6. They wanted security, **but** I wanted better pay.

7. There were more jobs up north, **and** I wanted one.

Practice 2 (page 35)

You may have used different coordinating conjunctions on some of the sentences. Have your instructor or a friend check your work.

1. I loved my home, **but** I had to leave.

2. I needed to find a new job, **or** my family wouldn't make it.

3. There were more jobs up north, **so** I moved to Detroit.

4. I found a job in an auto factory, **and** my income rose significantly.

5. The job paid extremely well, **so** I took it.
6. I was earning good money, **but** I still wanted to return to school.
7. I went back to school, **yet** I didn't quit my new job.
8. I worked days, my wife worked nights, **and** her mother watched the children on Saturdays.

ON THE OTHER HAND
Practice 2 (page 38)

You may have used different transitions. Have your instructor or a friend look over your work.

1. First,
2. Second,
3. For this reason,
4. However,
5. On the other hand,
6. On the whole,

Practice 3 (page 39)

1. The restaurant where Lucilla works is very busy. **For example,** it sells over 500 hot dogs on an average day.
   The restaurant where Lucilla works is very busy; **for example,** it sells over 500 hot dogs on an average day.
2. The building is shaped like a giant hot dog. **As a result,** the inside is very long and narrow.
   The building is shaped like a giant hot dog; **as a result,** the inside is very long and narrow.
3. It is hard to move around. The employees bump into each other constantly.
   It is hard to move around; the employees bump into each other constantly.
4. The owner refuses to air condition the building. **Therefore,** the employees who cook get very hot.
   The owner refuses to air condition the building; **therefore,** the employees who cook get very hot.
5. Lucilla doesn't have to cook. **On the other hand,** she does have to serve hot and surly customers.
   Lucilla doesn't have to cook; **on the other hand,** she does have to serve hot and surly customers.
6. Lucilla is tired of looking at all those hot dogs. **Furthermore,** she dreams about them every night.
   Lucilla is tired of looking at all those hot dogs; **furthermore,** she dreams about them every night.

Practice 4 (page 40)

1. Hector saw an attractive woman working behind the counter; consequently, he decided to talk to her.
2. She seemed bored with her job. She was, however, eager to talk to him.
3. OK
4. Lucilla was quite interested; for example, she asked him what kind of training volunteers received.
5. She had been looking for another job. She felt, on the other hand, that volunteer work might also make her life more meaningful.

I CAME, I SAW, I CONQUERED
Practice (page 42)

1. SS	5. CS	9. SS
2. CS	6. CS	10. SS
3. SS	7. SS	
4. CS	8. SS	

Proofread (page 43)

Here is how the corrected story should look.

I did not grow up in a wealthy family. My mother worked hard and barely made the monthly bills. We always had enough to eat, but dinners included a lot of rice and beans. My sister and I slept in the living room and studied at the kitchen table. My mother always encouraged us in our studies, and she checked our homework every night. My high school teachers also encouraged me, so I applied for a college scholarship. College was not easy, but I worked hard. I graduated and was hired by the National Insurance Company. I am now an account manager there. Hard work contributed to my success, but so did encouragement from my family and teachers.

SUPERIORITY COMPLEX
Practice 1 (page 45)

1. When Laura tried out for *West Side Story,* the director was thrilled.
2. Because the leading lady had quit, the director needed a new actress for the part of Maria.
3. Laura read the part after three other actresses had tried out.
4. The director wanted Laura for the part as soon as he heard her.

5. ⟨Although the others were more experienced,⟩ Laura had the right touch.

6. ⟨While the others could read lines more smoothly,⟩ Laura captured the spirit of Maria more vividly.

Practice 2 (page 45)

1. ⟨When⟩ Laura came home from her audition, her family wanted to know everything.

2. ⟨Although⟩ she didn't know for sure, she was hoping for the role of Maria.

3. Her family still had more questions ⟨after⟩ she had told them everything.

4. ⟨Before⟩ she had a chance to answer them, the phone rang.

5. The director called ⟨because⟩ he had some good news.

6. ⟨As soon as⟩ Laura hung up, she jumped for joy.

Practice 3 (page 46)

1. Before she got the part in *West Side Story*, she had never been in a play.
2. She had some preparation because she had once studied acting.
3. As soon as she got the script, she began to study her lines.
4. She felt upset when the director criticized her reading.
5. Because she saw her own improvement, she felt better.
6. She was terrified before the curtain went up.
7. Even though she was nervous, she remembered all her lines.
8. When the curtain went down, the audience went wild.

BECAUSE I SAID SO
Practice 2 (page 48)

You may have used slightly different subordinating conjunctions. Have your instructor or a friend look over your work.

1. We must believe in ourselves **even if** our friends don't believe in us.
   Even if our friends don't believe in us, we must believe in ourselves.

2. We must try our hardest **even though** we may feel like giving up.
   Even though we may feel like giving up, we must try our hardest.

3. We must finish our studies **although** they may be difficult.
   Although they may be difficult, we must finish our studies.

4. We must put up with criticism from disloyal friends **while** it may hurt our pride.
   While it may hurt our pride, we must put up with criticism from disloyal friends.

PIECES OF A COMPLEX WHOLE
Practice (pages 49-50)

1. frag	**4.** sent	**7.** frag	**10.** sent
2. sent	**5.** frag	**8.** sent	**11.** frag
3. frag	**6.** sent	**9.** sent	**12.** sent

Proofread (page 50)

When I was sixteen years old, I dropped out of school. I wasn't learning anything **because** I had lost interest. Although a few teachers reached out to me, **some** did not even pay attention to me in class. Because I wanted to belong somewhere, I joined a gang. Of course, I completely lost interest in school after I became a gang member. While life on the streets was tough, I couldn't imagine a different life and certainly didn't believe in any future. Then I got shot in a fight. While I was in the hospital, I had a lot of time to think. I had a choice between death in the streets and the chance for a new life in school. When I was eighteen years old, I enrolled in GED courses. Although sometimes I want to quit, I will try to make it this time.

MAKING COMPOUND FRACTURES
Practice 1 (pages 51-52)

You may have used different coordinating conjunctions. Have your instructor or a friend look over your work.

1. Personal stereos have earphones, **so** the sound enters the ear directly.
2. The sound drowns out other noises, **so** listeners can tune out their surroundings.
3. Some people use personal stereos on the bus, **or** they may use them at work.
4. Many people like to cover up outside sounds, **but** others find this distracting.
5. Personal stereos transmit sound only to the listener, **so** other people are not bothered by the noise.
6. Personal stereos offer many advantages, **yet** they have at least one disadvantage.

Practice 2 (pages 52-53)

You may have chosen different subordinating conjunctions. Have your instructor or a friend look over your work.

1. **When** her neighbors blast their radio, Karen can't concentrate.
2. **Although** some people love loud music, it can disturb others.
3. Some people get angry **when** others don't respect their need for quiet.
4. A few people like portable radios **because** the noise can keep other people away.
5. **When** some people play their music in a public place, they feel protected.
6. **Even though** portable radios are prohibited on buses in many cities, some people play them anyway.

Proofread (page 53)

You may have fixed these run-ons in a different way. Have your instructor or a friend check over your work.

We at Shady Towers want all our tenants to be satisfied, **so** we are presenting these rules:

1. Tenants should notify the management **if** they plan to have a party.
2. In their apartments, tenants should turn off all radios and stereos after 10:30 P.M. on weekdays, **and** they should turn them off by midnight on weekends.
3. Tenants must dispose of garbage properly. **Incinerators** should be used for this purpose.
4. Tenants may install air conditioners, **but** these air conditioners must be approved by the management.
5. Tenants may not use kerosene space heaters **because** these violate fire laws.
6. Tenants may use barbecue grills in the patio area. They may not bring the grills inside **because** this also violates fire laws.

COMPOUND AND COMPLEX SENTENCES

Practice (page 55)

1. **While** commercials are supposed to attract attention, many are ignored at first.
2. Commercials are supposed to attract attention, **but** many are ignored at first.
3. Commercials are supposed to attract attention. **However,** many are ignored at first. (OR . . . ; **however,** . . . .)
4. Most commercials are repeated frequently; **as a result,** people notice them eventually. (OR . . . frequently. **As a result,** . . . .)
5. Most commercials are repeated frequently, **so** people notice them eventually.

6. **Because** most commercials are repeated frequently, people notice them eventually.
7. **Although** people claim to ignore commercials, they are often influenced by them.
8. People claim to ignore commercials, **but** they are often influenced by them.
9. People claim to ignore commercials; **nevertheless,** they are often influenced by them. (OR . . . by them. **Nevertheless,** . . . .)

SHOW WHAT YOU KNOW
Proofread (page 56)

Here is an example of how the corrected passage might look. Yours may look different. Have your instructor or a friend look over your work.

To the Management:

We, the tenants of Shady Towers, are dissatisfied **with** the maintenance of our apartments **and** the public areas of the building. When the temperature dropped below freezing last winter, **the** radiators were not functioning. **As** a result, the apartments were intolerably cold. The pipes froze, they burst, **and** several apartments were flooded. The management has not paid for the damage to the furniture or the carpeting and curtains.

Furthermore, the hallways **are also a problem.** The doors to the incinerators are stuck on several floors, **so** the tenants must leave their garbage in the halls. **There** is nowhere else to put it.

Finally, the lobby **is very dangerous.** The locks on the outer doors are broken; **as a result,** hoodlums can get in and loiter by the elevators. Two tenants have been threatened, **and** they are now afraid to go in or out of the building.

Because the conditions of this building are dangerous and unlivable, we have consulted with a lawyer **and** with the Tenants' Rights Organization. We are prepared to take a series of legal steps. **However,** we will call them off **if** the management remedies the above-mentioned problems.

CHAPTER 3: SENTENCE BUILDING BLOCKS
PEOPLE, PLACES, THINGS, AND IDEAS
Practice 1 (page 59)

1. office, place
2. furniture, carpet
3. pictures, wall, windows

4. workers, boss, room
5. communication, management, employees
6. meetings, arguments
7. problems, situation, job

Practice 2 (page 60)

1. The management feels that the **International Bricklayers Union** should be prepared to make some concessions.
2. OK
3. A court-supervised repayment plan is almost always preferable to filing for bankruptcy, **Judge Macklin** has written.
4. My **psychiatrist** wants me to take a personality test.
5. According to Doctor Greenwood, this test will reveal much about my **unconscious thoughts**.
6. OK
7. My **mother** dislikes all of my friends.
8. OK

ONE POTATO, TWO POTATOES
Practice (page 61)

1. managers
2. workers
3. employees
4. boxes
5. typewriters
6. copies
7. machines
8. ideas

Proofread (page 62)

Some social service agencies give free help to **people** who have suffered financial and emotional **crises**. They may help families by finding them food, shelter, and clothing. They may work with husbands and **wives** who have had violent arguments. They may work with **children** whose **lives** have been disrupted by abuse. **Men, women**, and their **children** must meet several **criteria** to receive free help. They must show a need for help and a lack of ability to pay for it. **People** who work for these agencies do not achieve fame, but they are considered **heroes** by some of their clients.

WORKERS' COMPENSATION
Practice (pages 63-64)

1. employees'
2. employee's
3. managers'
4. president's
5. company's
6. companies'
7. people's
8. women's, men's

Proofread (page 64)

I belong to a union. My **union's** policies protect the workers in my industry. When a **worker's** rights are violated, he can speak to his representatives. To deal with the grievance, the **union's** representatives then speak with the **company's**. The union also protects workers as a whole. Of course, some unions have serious problems. There is a lot of corruption in some **unions'** leadership.

DIAMONDS AND RUST
Practice 1 (page 65)

1. bracelets
2. X
3. X
4. chairs
5. problems
6. X
7. X
8. dishes
9. children
10. X

Practice 2 (page 66)

1. much
2. a few
3. less
4. many
5. a few
6. much
7. several
8. fewer
9. These
10. A great deal
11. a number
12. This

YOU AND ME, BABE
Practice 1 (page 68)

1. **The doctor** [S] told **Stan** [O] what the test results were.
2. **She** [S] showed **the data** [O] that led her to diagnose diabetes.
3. **He** [S] asked many **questions** [O] about the disease.
4. After an hour, **Stan** [S] understood **the precautions** [O] he would need to take to stay healthy.
5. **The doctor** [S] reassured **him** [O] that he could live a normal life.
6. Next **Stan** [S] met with **the nurse** [O].
7. **She** [S] showed **him** [O] how to give himself insulin shots.
8. **He** [S] also learned about **blood sugar levels** [O] and how to measure them.
9. **Stan** [S] promised **himself** [O] to be very careful in his eating habits.
10. **He** [S] made **an appointment** [O] to come back in six weeks.

Practice 2 (page 69)

1. me
2. he   he
3. I   him
4. me
5. They
6. I   them
7. she   us
8. we   her
9. she
10. us

NOT OUR FAULT
Practice (page 72)

Here is how the corrected paragraph should look.

Roberto and Amanda had been working at **their** calculators all day. Unfortunately, **his** figures were not the same as **hers**. Amanda said, "I have an idea. You check **my** work, and I'll check **yours**." After twenty minutes, Roberto snapped his fingers and said, "**Your** work is fine, and so is **mine**. The calculators have done **their** job correctly, too. The problem is **our** boss. He gave one of us the wrong data to work on. Therefore, it was **his** mistake, not **ours**." "You're right," said Amanda. "Now, who wants to tell him?"

IT'S MY PARTY
Practice (pages 73-74)

1. He's
2. his
3. he's
4. your
5. you're
6. They're
7. their
8. its
9. your
10. it's
11. you're

Proofread (page 74)

Here is how the corrected paragraph should look.

Amanda Otero has worked in my department for several years now. Ms. **Otero's** work has been consistently diligent and reliable. She has frequently put in extra hours to fulfill the **company's** needs and has contributed significantly to **its** current healthy state. **She's** always conscientious about checking and correcting her own work. In addition, Ms. **Otero's** approach to her work has been innovative. **She's** able to analyze **situations** effectively even when **they're** not familiar to her. The result is fresh **solutions** to old problems. In fact, I have often reconsidered my own suggestions after hearing hers. Finally, she gets along well with her coworkers. She respects **their** views and is never afraid to say "**You're** right" to someone who points out a problem in her work. All in all, **it's** my pleasure to recommend a raise.

ME, MYSELF, AND I
Practice (pages 75-76)

1. OK
2. Shawn asked **himself** why he had failed at his first job.
3. The employees **themselves** contributed to their evaluations.
4. OK
5. OK
6. You and your family must take care of **yourselves** if all of you wish to remain healthy.
7. The people realized that they had brought disaster upon **themselves**.
8. Above all, we must be able to depend on **ourselves** if we want to succeed.

Proofread (page 76)

Here is how the corrected paragraph should look.

We must work hard to complete the Hastings project by the April deadline. The preparation itself will take several days, so we must allot two full weeks to the entire job. Selena and **I** will do the preparation, but we expect the rest of you to dedicate **yourselves** to the actual writing. William will be the one to present the report. Before his presentation, William must review it **himself**. Therefore, all participants must push **themselves** to verify every aspect of the report. If you have any questions, contact Selena or **me**.

THE GOOD, THE BAD, AND THE UGLY
Practice 1 (page 77)

1. Arizona has a warm climate.

2. Phoenix has high temperatures in the summer.

3. Phoenix has pleasant weather during the months of December, January, and February.

4. Phoenix is a popular center for tourists in the winter.

5. Near Phoenix, there are interesting places to visit.

6. Tourists can visit fascinating ruins left by the Hohokam Indians.

7. Visitors are awed by beautiful mountains.

QUICKLY BUT CAREFULLY
Practice 1 (page 80)

1. peacefully
2. kindly
3. quietly
4. noisily
5. fast
6. hard
7. angrily
8. well

FINE OR FINELY?
Practice 1 (pages 82-83)

1. tidy
2. neat
3. thoroughly
4. thorough
5. good
6. well
7. carefully
8. really

Proofread (page 83)

Here is how the corrected list should look.

Strengths

1. I am a **hard** worker.
2. I complete each task **thoroughly**.
3. I ask **intelligent** questions.
4. I am **really** enthusiastic about my work.
5. I am **helpful** to other workers.
6. I get along **well** with my superiors.

Weaknesses

1. I am **excessively** concerned with details.
2. I am very **serious**, even when others say I should take a situation **lightly**.
3. I tend to get angry too **easily**.
4. I often feel **insecure** about how others see me.

CHAPTER 4: VERB TENSES
TODAY AND EVERY DAY
Practice 1 (page 86)

1. eat
2. drinks
3. miss
4. feels
5. cooks   leaves
6. know   like
7. waits
8. understand   runs

Practice 2 (page 87)

1. do
2. goes
3. is
4. am
5. have
6. does
7. are

Practice 3 (page 88)

1. Where do you work?
2. Where does your wife work?
3. How much money do you earn?
4. How much money does your wife earn?
5. Why do you want this loan?
6. Why does she need a car?
7. Are you in debt to any other bank?

IT WAS ALL OVER
Practice 1 (page 89)

1. appeared
2. talked
3. answered
4. listened
5. discussed
6. reported

Proofread (page 91)

Here is how the corrected paragraph should look.

Did you **watch** "Rookie" on television last night? I **saw** it then for the first time, and I **didn't think** too much of it. I **was** so uninterested that I **went** out to make a sandwich. When I **came** back ten minutes later, the show **continued** to bore me. How **did** you **like** it? **Were** you bored, too?

COMING AND GOING
Practice (page 94)

The wording of your sentences may be slightly different. Have your instructor or a friend look over your work.

1. a. I was working on my project at this time yesterday.
   b. At this time tomorrow, I will be working on my project.
2. a. Tim was sleeping at nine o'clock last night.
   b. Tim will be sleeping when you come back from Virginia next week.
3. a. Right now you are shouting.
   b. As soon as you see that invoice, you will be shouting.
4. a. Even as we speak, Ms. Kim is waiting for her son.
   b. Last Tuesday at midnight, Ms. Kim was waiting for her son.
5. a. By the time the champagne is uncorked, the limousines will be arriving.
   b. The limousines were arriving by the time the chandeliers were installed.
6. a. The hairdresser was bleaching Samantha's hair as I passed by the salon.
   b. At this time tomorrow, the hairdresser will be bleaching Samantha's hair.

NOBODY'S PERFECT
Practice 2 (page 96)

1. has been
2. has been
3. has married
4. have stopped
5. has made
6. has begun
7. has worked
8. has gone
9. has taken
10. have indicated
11. has seen
12. has decided

Proofread (page 97)

Here is how the corrected paragraph should look.

David and Victor are inmates at Halsted Prison. So far, David **has** served two months, and Victor has **served** two years. Recently, both men **have been** studying in an education program at the prison called Project Workforce. Project

Workforce **has** been in effect for only a year at Halsted, but already over twenty volunteers from business and industry have been **helping** as tutors. In addition to attending state-sponsored vocational classes, inmates meet individually with their tutors several times per week. David says, "I have learned a lot in just a few weeks." Victor notes that they have **demanded** a lot of work, but he **hasn't given** up yet.

TIME HAD NOT STOOD STILL
Practice 1 (page 98)

1. had ended	**4.** had eaten
2. had left	**5.** had been
3. had drunk	**6.** had waited

Practice 3 (page 100)

1. got	had cashed
2. had	knew
3. walked	had bought
4. went	bought
5. decided	ate
6. had spent	left

DON'T TENSE UP
Practice 1 (page 101)

Here is how the corrected paragraph should look.

At the Martin Paper Company, I **have worked** as a receptionist for two years. I **answer** the telephone, **transfer** calls, and **give** out general information. I also **greet** visitors to the company and **notify** the proper persons of their arrival. This position **is** very satisfying because I **am** able to help the company function smoothly.

Practice 2 (page 102)

1. were	**4.** know	**7.** are
2. knew	**5.** have	**8.** have found
3. have learned	**6.** understand	**9.** will find

CHAPTER 5: OTHER VERB ISSUES
I'M NOT MISBEHAVING
Practice (page 105)

1. He **is not** telling the truth.
2. He **has not** told anyone the truth about the situation.
3. I **have not** heard whether or not anyone has discovered the actual facts.
4. He **is not** going to retain his current position.
5. We **are not** planning to encourage his behavior.
6. We **have not** gone to the proper authorities yet.
7. You **are not** being very helpful.

8. You **have not** been listening to what I've been saying.

MAKE NO BONES ABOUT IT
Practice 1 (page 106)

1. didn't
2. nothing
3. not   didn't
4. no
5. nobody   didn't
6. not   wouldn't
7. nothing
8. never
9. Neither

Proofread (page 107)

Here is an example of how the corrected paragraph might look. Yours may be slightly different.

Our neighbor Stella hadn't **ever** expected this surprise. She hadn't heard **any** of the stories about her new beau, Sidney. We had tried to tell her, but she would not listen to **any** of us. She always said, "I **haven't** paid attention to your stories before, and I **am not** going to start now." Sidney never told her **anything** about his marriage to Ma Bailey, the famous counterfeiter. He **said** nothing about his role in the bank robbery, **either**. When Ma Bailey came back to find her man, Stella **could** say not one word. She **had** never been so shocked. Finally, she opened her mouth and said, "Good-bye Sidney. You **aren't ever** going to see me again!"

WHAT IF . . . ?
Proofread (page 110)

Here is how the corrected skit should look.

LADY H: You are making a fool of yourself by flirting with the governess. If she **were** the slightest bit interested in you, I would be flabbergasted. Of course, you know that I **would** leave you here and now if I found the two of you together!

LORD H: My darling, rest assured that I love only you. If I **loved** the governess, I would ask you for a divorce this very day! You know I am an honest man!

LADY H: Oh, why did I marry you? If I had married the king, I would **have** been happy!

LORD H: Ah, but you are *not* a queen. Anyway, if the king **were** your husband, you'd still find something to complain about.

LADY H: If I **were** the queen, I would have no complaints. And now, dear man, you are giving me a royal pain. Be off!

YOU CAN QUOTE ME ON THAT
Practice 1 (page 111)
1. The senator said, "My constituents can have the fullest confidence that I will not vote against them."
2. She said, "The rebels are not supported by their own people, so they do not deserve our support."
3. The other senator added, "These so-called freedom fighters are simply glorified terrorists."
4. The vice president protested, "These men are fighting for democracy and are not terrorists."
5. The reporter asked, "Will this country continue to support the rebels?"

Practice 2 (page 112)
1. "The war is wrong," said the senator.
2. "What about the struggle for democracy?" asked the reporter.
3. The senator replied, "Democracy already exists in that land. The current president was elected by the people."
4. "That is simply not true," retorted the protest leader.
5. "What evidence do you have?" asked the reporter.

Practice 3 (page 113)
1. "The war," proclaimed the senator, "is wrong."
2. "I don't understand," she said. "Please explain your view."
3. "The people will win," said the protester. "We cannot keep them down."
4. "I support the rebels," said the vice president, "and so should all of us."
5. "I cannot agree with you," the senator replied. "This is an ill-advised policy."
6. "In the last few months," he said, "hundreds have fled."
7. "The living conditions were bad before," he added. "However, they are even worse now."
8. "Starvation and violence," said the volunteer, "are ravaging the population."
9. "We can do nothing," she continued. "We can only wait and watch."
10. "Although the situation is bad," she said, "there is still hope."

ACCURATE REPORTING
Practice 1 (page 115)
1. Ms. Park announced that she was ready to go.
2. She said that she had all of her notes.
3. She told Mr. Sulik that she had practiced her presentation several times.
4. Mr. Sulik noted that the audience would ask certain questions.
5. He promised that he would handle the difficult questions.
6. Ms. Park reassured him that she could answer them herself.
7. Ms. Park mentioned that she had written a list of possible questions.
8. Mr. Sulik told her that she was a valuable employee.

Practice 2 (page 116)
Your version may vary slightly. Have your instructor or a friend look over your work.

   I just overheard Alba and Zack carrying on and wasting time. First, Zack asked Alba where she wanted the boxes. Alba said that he could carry them up to the sixth floor. Zack asked her if she'd ever lifted an elephant. Then she told him he was a real comedian. Zack responded by asking her if she wanted to marry him, and Alba said that she would marry him on one condition. Zack asked what that was. She promised that she would tell him when he got back from the sixth floor.

CHAPTER 6: AGREEMENT
TIME OUT FOR INTERFERENCE
Practice 1 (page 119)
1. One disadvantage (of private policies) is the cost.
2. Group insurance (from employers) is less expensive.
3. Most people (in a large company) have group insurance.
4. Frequently, people (who do part-time work) lack insurance benefits.
5. A person (without insurance benefits) needs to pay for a private policy.
6. Individuals (who cannot afford private insurance) suffer when they have to pay medical bills.

Practice 2 (page 120)
1. OK
2. Many people without insurance **avoid** medical care.

3. A person who has no insurance benefits **suffers** from high bills or bad medical care.
4. A company that offers insurance benefits **provides** a real service to its employees.
5. OK
6. One disadvantage of part-time jobs **is** the lack of insurance benefits.
7. OK
8. Medical bills even for a minor injury **are** often surprisingly high.
9. OK
10. Unfortunately, paperwork that must go through many channels **slows** the process down.

ALL IS NOT ONE
Practice 1 (page 122)
1. has
2. doesn't
3. appreciate
4. likes
5. argue
6. Does
7. is   resolves
8. refuses
9. works

Practice 3 (page 123)
1. was
2. were
3. was
4. was
5. was
6. were

Proofread (pages 123-124)
Here is how the corrected paragraph should look.

Our washer and dryer are broken beyond repair. Neither **is** fixable within our budget. Therefore, all of us **are** going to have to pitch in to get the laundry done by other methods. Each of us **needs** to volunteer one night a week to go to the laundromat. Nobody **likes** to drag big bags of clothes to a laundromat, I know, so if some of the wash **gets** done every night, everyone will have to do just one or two loads. A few of the things **don't** need to be machine washed. For instance, most of the underwear only **has** to be soaked in hot, soapy water, and each of Jeroma's many sweaters is better off anyway if hand washed. If someone **has** a problem with helping with the laundry, all of his or her things **stay** in the laundry hamper. I need all of you to cooperate. If everyone **helps**, we can keep our household running smoothly.

NEWS FOR THE PUBLIC
Practice 1 (page 126)
1. has
2. need
3. are
4. become
5. is
6. is
7. need
8. does

AND/OR
Practice (page 128)
1. depend
2. has
3. are
4. need
5. requires
6. is
7. are

HERE COMES TROUBLE
Proofread (page 130)
Here is how the corrected letter should look.

Dear Sir or Madam:

The Robo-Butler that we purchased last week is defective. First, there **are** no instructions telling us how to operate the robot. In addition, there **is** only one mechanical arm instead of the three arms pictured in the ad. Finally, on the mechanical arm, there are only two fingers instead of five, and on one of the fingers **is** a broken joint.

For four days, we have tried unsuccessfully to telephone your toll-free number. The first time there was a busy signal, next there **was** a recorded message, and then for the last three days there **has** been no answer whatsoever. For this reason, we are writing a letter in the hope of a quick response. Please remember that there **are** many people dependent upon your robot service for three meals a day and a clean house!

Here **is** all the information you will need. Our Robo-Butler (Serial No. 53212-6) was purchased at Robot Shack in San Diego, California, on May 21 for $799.99. Enclosed **are** the receipts from the store and the credit company.

Thank you for your prompt attention.

SHOW WHAT YOU KNOW
Proofread (pages 131-132)
Here is how the corrected passage should look.

Cassandra and her trusted companion Eloise **were** in mortal fear. The robber band **was** drawing closer by the minute. Soon, either Cassandra or Eloise **was** going to have to jump from the hiding place in the cliff to the swirling depths below.

Finally, Cassandra spoke. "You and I **are** in this together. No one **is** going to rescue us, so we must make a plan. Now, in my satchel **are** two pieces of rope. Tie them together and then lower me down to the sea."

"Yes, my lady," murmured Eloise, fumbling with the rope.

"Speak up, woman!" cried Cassandra.

"Your murmurs and whispers **are** starting to get on my nerves. If you do not help me, everything **is** lost!"

"All of my hopes and wishes **go** with you," Eloise said, a new determination in her voice. With that, she tied the rope around Cassandra's waist, and Cassandra slipped over the edge.

She hit the water and began to swim with all her strength. Suddenly, she looked up from the frothy waves. A boat with two men **was** making its way toward her. "My companion and I **have** come to save you!" one of the men **was** shouting.

"Dirk! Blithers! Thank goodness it is you!" she exclaimed as the two men pulled her into the boat.

Then she went on, "My news **is** not good. The robbers are after us. I jumped to get help, but Eloise **remains** above, cold and hungry."

Cassandra looked around. In the boat **were** warm clothes and other provisions. "Here **are** some sandwiches, my lady," said Blithers. "Eat hearty."

As she ate, she looked toward shore. "There **is** another person in the waves!" she cried. " 'Tis Eloise."

Moments later, both pairs of lovers **were** reunited. Each of the ladies **was** with her man. Their clothes **were** in rags and they had no money, but they **were** happy. "The poor **are** blessed when they are with the ones they love," said Dirk. He set sail, and the boat drifted to safety.

WHO IS HE?
Practice 1 (page 134)

Indoor gardening is an excellent hobby for people with busy and stressful lives. Moreover, while plants can provide hours of pleasure and relaxation, they do not require a lot of attention. Daily water and a place in the sun are their only requirements. In return, each plant brightens its own little corner of the house. Plants do more than just decorate, however. Many plant owners report that they feel calmer and more peaceful when they water their plants or simply gaze at them.

Practice 2 (page 135)
1. Plants bring long-lasting pleasure to **their** owners.
2. A cactus requires a lot of sun but little water. Be extremely careful not overwater **it**.
3. OK
4. My family and I have a virtual jungle in **our** living room.
5. If a plant requires bright sun, do not place **it** in a dark corner of the house.
6. OK
7. A little boy of seven, for instance, could be taught to take care of **his** own plant independently.
8. OK
9. Sometimes plant lovers inadvertently kill one of their green companions. In this situation, **they** mourn the loss of **their** plant almost as **they** would mourn the loss of a beloved pet.

Practice 3 (pages 136-137)
1. Some of the plants had lost **their** leaves.
2. OK
3. My scissors lost **their** sharpness from cutting off all the dead leaves.
4. OK
5. Each plant had something wrong with **its** leaves.
6. All of the soil needed water right away—**it** felt bone-dry.
7. Neither cactus looks as though **it** had trouble.
8. OK
9. Either Freddie or Willie forgot to water the plants while I was away. When I find out who it was, I will yell at **him** (or **her**).

SHOW WHAT YOU KNOW
Proofread (page 138)
Here is how the corrected passage should look.

Most **houseplants** die from incorrect watering. If you neglect to water them regularly, **they** will die a rapid death. On the other hand, if **you overwater** them, they will die slowly as they turn yellow and the leaves drop from the stems.

How do you know how much water to use? The answer depends in large part on the plants **themselves**. You need to read enough about each plant to know how frequently it requires water. If you have a cactus or a succulent, for example, you should water **it** very infrequently. However, if you have **ferns**, you may need to water **them** daily.

Feeding is another important issue.

Determining how much fertilizer a plant needs can be tricky. The directions on many commercial fertilizers recommend too frequent feeding, so **you'd** do best to ignore **them.** Instead, use the instructions given by a reputable plant-care book.

Our next issue will be loaded with news—some of **it** good and some of **it** bad—for plants with pest problems. Learn which plants can be saved and which must be laid to rest.

CHAPTER 7: MODIFIERS AND PARALLEL STRUCTURE
PEOPLE WHO NEED PEOPLE
Practice (page 141)

1. Amateur photographers are people **who** take pictures for pleasure.
2. Professional photographers are people **who** earn money for their camera work.
3. A camera **which** develops its own photos is called a self-developer.
4. Photographers **who** work in portrait studios earn a steady income.
5. The room **which** is used to develop photographs is called a darkroom.
6. There are a number of magazines **which** specialize in photography.
7. Professionals and amateurs **who** buy these magazines can improve their techniques.
8. Some amateurs join clubs **which** encourage members to share new photography techniques.

FOR WHOM THE BELL TOLLS
Practice 1 (page 143)

1. whom
2. who
3. whom
4. whom
5. who

THE MAN WHO KNEW TOO MUCH
Practice (page 144)

1. The woman **who knew CPR** hurried to the scene of the accident.
2. The man **who had the heart attack** was very lucky to have survived.
3. The stricken man was surrounded by people **who watched helplessly.**
4. Someone remembered that he had a friend **who knew CPR** and hurried to find her.
5. The woman **who saved the man's life** had just been trained in CPR the week before.
6. The ambulance **that finally arrived on the scene** had been stuck in a traffic jam.

7. The ambulance took the man to a hospital **that was located only blocks away,** and an emergency team went to work on him right away.

ADJECTIVE CLAUSES
Proofread (page 146)

Here is how the corrected passage should look.

Monday, March 28

Security Guard Mendoza reported a suspicious finding in the safe-deposit area. She saw a safe-deposit box **that (or which)** had been left open. Moments later, the bank patron **who was renting the box** returned and explained that he had had to step out for a moment to use the restroom.

Wednesday, March 30

Security Guard Fredriks was approached by a woman **who** said she had just been robbed of ten dollars after using the automatic teller machine. Upon questioning, the woman revealed that it was her husband **who** had taken the money. She was afraid he intended to buy cigarettes with the money and wanted the guard to prevent him. Fredriks said he could do nothing. The woman shouted a few words **which I do not care to print** and marched out.

Friday, April 1

Security Guard Fredriks reported an incident **that (or which)** aroused his suspicion. He saw a man who seemed to be wearing a disguise enter the bank. The man, in fact, was dressed as an old woman, and in his coat pocket there was a large bulge **that (or which)** appeared to be a gun. Fredriks approached the man and asked him to show the contents of the pocket. The man took out a large sweet potato **that (or which)** had sprouts growing from it and offered it to Fredriks. Fredriks said he was about to contact the supervisor **who** had just come on duty when the man said, "Look at the date, fool!" and ran out of the bank.

IN THE LAUNDROMAT
Practice (page 148)

1. Ricky stared at the long row of dryers **against the wall.**
2. Lucy carefully measured out the bleach **in the cup.**
3. Ricky was annoyed to find "out of order" signs **on most of the dryers.**
4. They began to fold the wet clothes **in the basket.**
5. The attendant **behind the counter** refused to give them any change.

6. **In an unpleasant voice,** the attendant asked Ricky not to smoke his cigar. OR
The attendant asked Ricky **in an unpleasant voice** not to smoke his cigar.

STAYING CLOSE
Practice (page 149)
Your sentences may vary slightly. Have your instructor or a friend look over your work.
1. I had to attend to the **kicking and screaming** baby.
2. **Worried about the baby,** I almost called the doctor.
3. I tried to lift the infant **struggling against me.**
4. He cried for his teddy bear **sitting on a tall shelf.**
5. **Striding into the room,** his mother saw him.
6. **Reaching for her,** he put his arms around her neck.
7. She smiled at the baby, **now sleeping soundly.**

THE DANGLING CONVERSATION
Practice (page 151)
Your rewritten sentences may look different from these. Have your instructor or a friend look over your work.
1. Looking out the window, I saw the man on the street run up behind the woman.
2. He grabbed her purse and ran while she screamed for help.
3. As he was running down the street, I picked up the telephone and dialed the police.
4. Back at the window again, I saw that the woman had jumped up and was chasing her attacker.
5. She caught up with the man, who seemed amazed at the woman's speed.
6. Grabbing him by the hood of his jacket, she made him lose his balance.
7. The woman kicked the startled man, who fell to the ground.
8. The man shielded his head and begged for mercy from the woman standing menacingly above him.
9. The man yielded up the stolen pocketbook to the victorious woman.

MAKING THE IDENTIFICATION
Practice 1 (pages 152-153)
1. Judge Howard, **once a respected man in the community,** had accepted bribes and payoffs.
2. The newspapers vilified Judge Howard, **once a respected man in the community.**
3. The Cedar Valley *News,* **which had**

previously endorsed the judge,** published a scathing editorial against him.
4. The judge was supported only by the *Midnight Mind,* **a local scandal sheet.**
5. The *Midnight Mind,* **not known for its journalistic excellence,** had reportedly accepted money from the judge.
6. The town's only high school, **which the judge had attended in his youth,** took down the judge's picture.
7. The judge was the butt of several jokes on "Komedy Tonight", **a comedy show on the local cable station.**

Practice 2 (page 154)
1. OK
2. Harvey Whiteglove, who represented the judge in court, had a "Mr. Clean" reputation.
3. Bribery, a very serious crime, cannot be tolerated in our judicial system.
4. Martin Lawless, an attorney long suspected of corruption, was one of many participants in the scheme.
5. OK
6. Judge Howard received a ten-year sentence, a stiff and unforgiving penalty.
7. OK
8. OK
9. Halsted Penitentiary, located near the southern border of the state, will be the judge's new home.
10. We need to renew our faith in the judicial system, a system based on honesty and trust.

Proofread (page 155)
Here is how the corrected paragraph should look.

Judge Howard, once a respected community leader, has been found guilty of corruption. The trial that he received was a fair one, and the evidence presented at the trial was overwhelming. Judge Howard has undermined our faith in the judicial system, a system in which we all must trust. What motivated Judge Howard? Was his salary, which had just risen to $50,000, insufficient? Was his need for a car with reclining leather seats and a wet bar undeniable? We think not. Judge Howard was motivated by greed, the ugliest of sins. Any judge who is motivated by greed cannot be an upholder of justice. We applaud the decision made by the court. We applaud the sentence received by the judge. And we applaud Cedar Valley, a community of decent and hardworking people, for its adherence to the highest standards of honesty and justice.

KEEPING EACH LINE STRAIGHT
Practice 1 (page 157)

There is often more than one way to make the structures parallel. Have your instructor or a friend look over your work.

1. My job pays poorly and **provides** no benefits.
2. OK
3. I often fantasize about being rich and **buying** a Mercedes.
4. A Mercedes is a luxury car **and** a status symbol. **It** sends a message about its owner.
5. OK
6. Unfortunately, I can't afford to buy or **maintain** even a Yugo.
7. A new job with better benefits and **good pay** must be my first priority.
8. I have experience **and** expertise. I deserve a position in a good company.
9. OK
10. Perhaps I will never be able to buy or **drive** a Mercedes.
11. However, **owning** a small car and earning a decent income are realistic goals for me.

Practice 2 (page 158)

There is often more than one way to make the structures parallel. Have your instructor or a friend look over your work.

1. The lawyer was a woman **who had** a sharp mind and who made shrewd decisions.
2. She wanted to know our names, **our addresses,** and our phone numbers.
3. She also requested to know where we worked and **what our schedules were**.
4. We were people who knew nothing of the law and **had** an ingrained mistrust of the legal profession.
5. The lawyer was quite expensive but **proved** very competent.
6. We were satisfied with her handling of our case and **the outcome of the trial**.

INDEX